"I have would ju[...] [...]n very pleasantly surprised to find a great deal of valuable information." ***Brian Bissell***

"I would highly recommend Paul's book…to anyone who is considering purchasing property on the lake. It answers not only the obvious questions but also details many items (like dock permits) that a novice lake buyer would not think to ask." ***Suzy & Dave Barta***

"Paul Moore's book on buying property on SML is a must read." ***Linda & Judd Riedinger***

"I just wish we had been exposed to this kind of education about SML before we made our purchase!" ***Robert Harbert***

"We have never seen a real estate agent that supplied so much information… It is all so informative and helpful in our hunt for a home at SML." ***Charles & Gladys Impink***

"Thank you for this information, this is a great book that you have assembled!!! I have never seen such effort from a real estate agent." ***Will Rogers, Jr.***

"Your book is extremely helpful to both buyers and your realty staff." *Scott from NJ*

"We will be happy to pass your name along as a referral to anyone interested in moving to the lake. Your book tells volumes about your knowledge and my husband and I would not hesitate to recommend you so that anyone interested in coming into the area may avoid some of the issues we ran into, some of which were costly and time consuming. Most of the issues would have been avoided had we read your book first." *Carol Ridgely*

"Paul's book is a must read for anyone considering relocating to or purchasing a vacation home or investment property at SML. He is a dear friend, and I have co-owned a house with him and co-invested in properties with him at SML for years. He is the real deal; read his book and learn from him. You will not be disappointed!" *Dr. Austin Spruill*

The Definitive Guide to Smith Mountain Lake Real Estate

3rd Edition

Paul Moore

Copyright © 2008, 2012 & 2016

Paul Moore – REALTOR®
All Rights Reserved

All rights reserved. No part of this book may be reproduced in any form, except for the inclusion of brief quotations in a review, without permission in writing from the author or publisher.

Library of Congress
Control Number: 2008901283

Additional copies of this book are available on Amazon.com® or by contacting the author at

SmithMountainHomes.com
1-877-SML-HOME
P.O. Box 7301
Roanoke, VA 24019

Published by Paul Moore

Cover Photos by Eric and Shannon Grierson

Edited & Updated by Carole McFarland, Larry Pierce, Carrie Thompson & Doug & Holly Nicholson

Cover Design by Esther Joy & Savanna Kahle

Third Edition

Table of Contents

Acknowledgements 11

Introduction to This Guide 13

Section I: Introduction to Smith Mountain Lake 15
   The Crown Jewel of the Blue Ridge 17
   Smith Mountain Lake Quick Facts 19
   Overview of Smith Mountain Lake 21
   How Do I Start My Lake Property Search? 33

Section II: Assessing SML Property Values 39
   How is Smith Mountain Lake Waterfront Property Valued? Seven Key Factors 41
   What is the Quality of the Water at Smith Mountain Lake? Does Water Quality Affect Property Values? 48
   How Does Water Depth Affect My Lake Experience and Property Value? 49
   How Does the Rising and Falling Water Level Affect My Experience at Smith Mountain Lake? 50
   Can I Dredge in Front of My Property to Get Deeper Water? 51
   What is Riprap Anyway? What Options Do I Have to Control Erosion in Front of My Waterfront Property? 53
   Can I Have a Dock? What about a Full Boathouse? 55
   Can I Get a Beach? 61
   Can I Cut Down or Trim Trees to Improve My View? 62
   What Restrictions May I Face From Homeowner Associations? 67
   What is a Water-Access Home? 68

Section III: SML Investment Properties 69
   I Want to Rent Out My Home. Are All SML Homes Rentable? 71
   How Do I Find the Perfect Rental Home? 72

Is There Cash Flow Potential from a Waterfront Rental Home?... 77

Section IV: The Ideal Waterfront Lot............................... **79**
Finding the Perfect Waterfront Lot. How Are Lots Valued?.. 81
Should I be Concerned About a Septic System?................ 86
Can I Split my Waterfront Property into Multiple Parcels?.. 88

Section V: Building A New Home..................................... **91**
I Want to Build a Home. Is There an Ideal Mountain-Lake Home Style?.. 93
How Close to the Water Can I Build My New Home?........ 94
Is it Tough to Obtain a Building Permit at SML?................ 98
Building a Home: What Will It Cost? How Long Will It Take?... 99
Building a Home: What About Modular Homes?............. 101
Building a Home: Should I Add a Basement or a Garage?... 104
How Do I Design My Basement for Maximum Enjoyment and Resale Value?... 106
Building a Home: How Do I Find a Contractor?............... 108
Building a Boathouse or Dock: What Will It Cost?.......... 115
How Do I Finance My New Home Construction?............ 117
Can I Build Multiple Homes on One Property? Can I Build a Guesthouse on My Property?................................ 118

Section VI: Purchasing Property at SML........................ **119**
I Can't Afford It… Or Can I? Some Creative Ways to Finance a Waterfront Home at Smith Mountain Lake 121
Seller and Buyer, Sittin' in a Tree…What is a Love Letter? Should I Write One? Why and How?.................... 126
Do I Need a Home Inspection?... 128
Do I Need a Property Survey?... 131
I Want to Buy a Home at the Lake, but I Dread Paying for Flood Insurance. Will I Need it?....................................... 133

How is the Dock Transferred to the New Owner at
Closing?.. 134
How Do I Close on my Smith Mountain Lake Property?.. 136

Section VII: Choosing a REALTOR® at SML 141
Do I Really Need a REALTOR® to Acquire My SML
Dream Home?... 143
Choosing a REALTOR® for Your SML Transaction 147
Choosing a Buyer's Agent at Smith Mountain Lake........... 149
Selling Your Home? Special Considerations in Selecting
a Listing Agent at Smith Mountain Lake 152

**Section VIII: Smith Mountain Lake – A Great Place to
Own Real Estate!... 161**
What Amenities, Accommodations & Entertainment Does
Smith Mountain Lake Offer?... 163
How Does the Cost of Living Compare to Other Areas
of the United States? 166
How is the Weather at Smith Mountain Lake? Do You
Have Hurricanes Like Other Waterfront Destinations? 167
I Love to Sail or Want to Learn. Are there Areas of the
Lake that are Better for Sailing?... 168
Is There a Warm Side Versus a Cold Side of this Lake? ... 169
How Could Global Warming Affect Vacation Properties in
the U.S.? How Will this Affect Smith Mountain Lake?..... 170
Is Smith Mountain Lake a Profitable Place to Invest? 173
Smith Mountain Lake Versus the Beach 176
Come to the Mountains 179

Appendices 181
Appendix A: A Brief History of Smith Mountain Lake 183
Appendix B: How Electricity is Produced at Smith
Mountain Lake.. 188
Appendix C: From You to SML - Drive Times &
Distances... 190
Appendix D: Smith Mountain Lake in the National
Media 191

Appendix E: When Smith Mountain Lake Won't Satisfy .. 198
Appendix F: The Dreamer's Challenge 201

About the Author 207

A Special Offer for SML Home Buyers 209

A Special Offer for SML Home Sellers 211

Acknowledgements

The Scriptures say that the heavens and the earth give glory to the Creator. Smith Mountain Lake, though created by the ingenuity of men, gives great honor to the Creator of water, earth and sky. I thank Him for giving me the opportunity to work here and for the joy of being His friend.

I want to thank Elaine, my wonderfully supportive and patient wife of 29 years, and my four extraordinary children, Jonathon, Hannah, Mary and Abby.

I want to enthusiastically thank the Smith Mountain Homes Realty Team and Staff. You are the best!

I want to thank my fellow REALTORS® from all of the great brokerages here at Smith Mountain Lake. I have learned so much from you and enjoyed getting to know you along the way. Thanks!

Introduction to this Guide

Before I became a buyer's agent at Smith Mountain Lake, I worked with a wide variety of buyers and sellers in Roanoke and the surrounding area. I also bought and sold a substantial number of properties of my own in Virginia, Michigan and Ohio. Through this process, I learned that there is usually a homogeneity within a neighborhood or area that allows properties to be valued using relatively consistent criteria such as the state of repair of the home and yard, the view, the interior features, and the construction. These factors exert a predictable influence on the assessment of a property. The saying is usually true...the big issue is Location, Location, Location!

With this understanding in mind, my investment group began to purchase foreclosed properties at courthouse step auctions after merely driving by the home and checking comparable values in the neighborhood. We learned that there is *usually* not a huge cost difference between remodeling a somewhat dated home and a significantly neglected or trashed home. We were able to learn from a real estate trainer how to give a home valuation estimate over the phone after asking the owner only their address and a few additional questions.

When I began to work at the lake, however, things weren't nearly so simple. Because of the significant number of critical variables for any given property, it would be virtually unthinkable for even a seasoned local agent to precisely evaluate a waterfront home or lot without a thorough personal inspection. At a place where a shabby trailer often sells for more than a nice new contemporary home, and a waterfront lot is sometimes more than double the price of the home built on it, it is clear that the rules are different here. The complexity of issues related to view, slope, waterfront, water depth, water quality, location on the channel or cove, rentability, permissibility for a dock, septic regulations and much more mean that it is *critical* for a buyer here to really understand the factors that drive the value and the functionality of a given property. It is my hope that this guide will serve that function.

My team and I have worked with many buyers and sellers on the lake, and we have found that there are a number of frequently asked questions they pose when they are considering buying a property. There is also information we share with them that they wouldn't know to ask about. This guide is organized along the lines of these typical questions and issues. Most of the sections start with a question.

Answers to many of the questions can only be guidelines as you anticipate your property search through a licensed real estate agent. There are many fantastic agents here at Smith Mountain Lake, and this guide cannot begin to replace the assistance that they provide. I hope that it will, however, provide you with a start on your treasure hunt at the Crown Jewel of the Blue Ridge, Smith Mountain Lake!

SECTION I:

Introduction to Smith Mountain Lake

What's in This Section?

The Crown Jewel of the Blue Ridge

Smith Mountain Lake Quick Facts

Overview of Smith Mountain Lake

How Do I Start My Lake Property Search?

The Crown Jewel of the Blue Ridge

Smith Mountain Lake has quickly become one of the most popular destinations for vacationers, second-homeowners, retirees and telecommuters in the Eastern United States. The lake is a natural draw for water and mountain lovers of all sorts. Home Buyers from New England to the West Coast have come to Smith Mountain Lake. Many simply have located Smith Mountain Lake on a map, scheduled a trip, and had a property deed in hand a month later. The water and mountains here seem to have an irresistible draw. Some comment that they have traveled throughout the United States and have never seen a more beautiful spot.

Consider the Pennsylvania school principal and his wife, a teacher. They had grown up on the water in New Jersey and had been saving up for 38 years to retire there. They had been on an unsuccessful 2½-year search all over the East Coast for the perfect spot. After locating Smith Mountain Lake on a map one December, they scheduled a three-day trip over Christmas break. They were overwhelmed by the beauty of the mountains, the water, and the quaint rural surroundings. Within a month they closed on a beautiful waterfront lot and have recently moved into their dream retirement home.

Or consider the Silicon Valley executive and his wife. As they began to plan for retirement recently, they considered the places they had lived and visited all over the United States and the world. They considered both coasts and many spots in between, but remembered a brief stop they had once made in Southwestern Virginia. During a four-day trip, Scott toured the lake by boat, car and plane. On day-four he made his decision and he and his wife are now the owners of their fantasy waterfront property. They will call it home permanently when they retire.

From the D.C. attorney who bought property on his first day at the lake, to the family who bought a cottage on their trip back north from Florida, the stunning beauty and abundance of

Section I: Introduction to Smith Mountain Lake

property as well as the many quality-of-life factors have made Smith Mountain Lake a magnet for people who love the Blue Ridge Mountains, clean water, fresh air and water sports.

Yet this rush to buy lots and homes here has meant problems for some buyers. Smith Mountain Lake, like all waterfront destinations, has a number of issues that, if ignored, can have serious repercussions for property values and quality of life. Fortunately, each of these issues can be navigated successfully with good counsel and careful investigation. This guide is designed to be the first step in that process. Through carefully following the advice here, you should be able to confidently move forward in buying the property of your dreams here at Smith Mountain Lake.

Please note that this document should only be used as a guideline. Laws and rulings can and do change, and it is possible that some of the rules quoted in the following pages may be outdated by the time you purchase a property here and are ready to build or expand. Though I have reviewed it repeatedly for accuracy, it is also possible that I have made mistakes along the way. Please contact a professional local realty agent and/or the appropriate local authority in the areas in which you have questions.

The Definitive Guide to Smith Mountain Lake Real Estate

SMITH MOUNTAIN LAKE QUICK FACTS

Shoreline: 500+ miles

Main Channel: Approximately 40 miles

Elevation: 795 feet above sea level at lake

Local Population: Approximately 20,000

Nearby Cities: Roanoke – Under one hour. Area population approx. 290,000*

Lynchburg – Under one hour. Area population approx. 240,000*

Greensboro/High Point/Winston-Salem Approximately 1.5+ hours.

Blacksburg/Virginia Tech – 1.5 hours

Charlottesville – 2 hours

Raleigh-Durham/Chapel Hill – 2+ hours.

Climate: Mild, enjoyable temperatures during the four distinct seasons. Summer temperatures average in the upper 70s. Water temperatures average 70 degrees from May to October. The average annual snowfall is less than 18 inches. With four distinct seasons, the lake has the welcome absence of a mosquito population. Near perfect!

Section I: Introduction to Smith Mountain Lake

Counties: Franklin, Bedford and Pittsylvania Counties

*Area populations are drawn from U.S. Census Data as reported in Wikipedia.org. Census data is of the metropolitan area, which includes the city itself, as well as portions of several surrounding counties.

Overview of Smith Mountain Lake

Before launching into more detail about real estate at Smith Mountain Lake, some readers may want a broad-brush version of the lake as a whole. Smith Mountain Lake was formed in the 1960's as a power generation project of Appalachian Power, part of American Electric Power (AEP). It is the result of a 235-foot tall dam in a gap of Smith Mountain on the Roanoke River channel in Pittsylvania County (see Appendix "A Brief History of Smith Mountain Lake" for more details about how this came about).

The main channels of the lake total about 40 miles along the basins of two main rivers, the Roanoke and the Blackwater, which join a few miles west of the dam and flow together to form the widest part of the lake. The Roanoke River channel flows south-southeast from the city of Roanoke to the lake, and it generally provides a border between Franklin County on the southwest and Bedford County on the northeast shore. The Blackwater River Channel generally flows west to east through Franklin County until it joins the Roanoke River Channel near the Pittsylvania County border. At the point where the main channels join, the combined main channel flows east to the dam and provides a border between Bedford County on the north and Pittsylvania County on the south shore.

In addition to the two main channels, there are numerous other tributaries that were backed up as a result of the dam at Smith Mountain. Since the dam provided a water level at 795 feet above sea level along all of these creeks and stream basins, several creeks are as broad in places as parts of the main channel itself. Those familiar with the lake throw around the names of tributaries as though they are talking about separate entities from the lake. Comments such as "try out that Marina on the east side of Craddock Creek" or "the striper bass are really running near the mouth of Betty's Creek" may seem confusing to newcomers, but you'll quickly become accustomed to the local lingo. Some of the main tributaries in Bedford

Section I: Introduction to Smith Mountain Lake

County are Witcher Creek, Hatcher Creek and Craddock Creek. Major tributaries in Franklin County include Bull Run, Betty's Creek, Becky's Creek, Gill's Creek, Lynville Creek and several more.

Navigation

One of the many wonderful features of Smith Mountain Lake is the numbered navigation channel marker system on both the main channels and the tributaries. The Roanoke Channel numbers start at R1 near the dam and extend west, then north/northwest, toward Roanoke, ending with R80 near the Hardy Bridge. The Blackwater Channel and all other marked channels are numbered starting at the point where they join the main channel and work up from there. C1, for example, would be the first marker where Craddock Creek joins the Roanoke Channel near the chain of three islands northwest of the dam. As boaters proceed up through the C series, they would be progressing north on Craddock Creek to its end at C8 near Mariner's Landing. Not only are the channel markers numbered, but they are color-coded and lighted for navigational ease. Red and green lights guide a boater through the center of the channel on a dark night, and the numbers make it easy to stay on course by day. With a map in hand, this system makes Smith Mountain Lake a prime place to fish by day or night year-round. I have taken many clients and friends out to dinner by boat and returned home with relative ease late at night. A few years back, my wife and I enjoyed the full August moon rising over Smith Mountain by boat before midnight on her birthday. It would have been challenging making this beautiful memory without the wonderful navigational marker system. A smartphone or boat-mounted GPS system work great here, showing the details of channels, coves and inlets across our vast mountain lake.

Shoreline
Though Smith Mountain Lake has only about 40 miles of main river channels, it boasts an impressive 500+ miles of total shoreline. This figure is staggering as one considers that this is the approximate highway distance from here to New York City! This shoreline figure is a testimony to the many large tributaries that flow into the lake as well as the lovely, rolling nature of the Blue Ridge Mountain terrain that makes up Smith Mountain Lake's borders. This terrain gives Smith Mountain Lake many hundreds of coves, inlets, twists and turns that make for breathtaking views, marvelous home sites, and practically unlimited spots to anchor a boat for a picnic lunch, swim, watch a romantic sunset, or catch a double-digit weight striped bass.

Islands
In addition to its many coves and inlets, the rolling Blue Ridge Mountain terrain has provided Smith Mountain Lake with many lovely islands. These islands are formed from old mountaintops or ridgelines. A few of these islands are privately owned but most are available for the public's enjoyment. Boaters regularly anchor their crafts offshore, providing a place for kids to wade in the sand and swim. Some stop for a picnic lunch or explore the trails. Many people have found great fishing holes off island shores.

Counties
As I mentioned earlier, Smith Mountain Lake is surrounded by three mountainous, rural counties: Bedford, Franklin and Pittsylvania. As you consider purchasing real estate here at Smith Mountain Lake, it will be important for you to know how these counties differ. Though most of our clients don't come here with a particular county or section of the lake in mind, many of them develop an affinity for a particular county or section as they spend time here looking at property. One reason for a buyer to select a particular county would be their desire to

Section I: Introduction to Smith Mountain Lake

rent or not rent their home out on a short-term basis. We will cover this in detail later.

One caveat about this section: It is difficult to be completely accurate when generalizing about a particular county's waterfront property. Much of what can be said about one county can be said about all three. Are you looking for a county with cozy vacation cottages? You can find them in all three counties. Are you seeking a newer, multi-million dollar luxury waterfront home? They are also available in all three counties. Are you trying to find (or avoid) an old trailer on a waterfront lot? All three counties have some left. Searching for a condo? A piece of land to subdivide? A huge point with lots of privacy? All are available in all three counties. Most of the lake offers wonderful property, beautiful vistas, deep water and great home sites. With this caveat in mind, here are a few comments and generalizations about each county.

Bedford County

Bedford County encompasses the northern and eastern shore of the lake. The Bedford County shoreline, from north to south, includes addresses in Goodview, Moneta and Huddleston. Bedford County allows vacation and long-term rentals, and the vast majority of waterfront rentals on the lake are here. There are about 3,200 waterfront property owners in Bedford County, according to the county tax records. This includes homes, townhomes, condos, lots and land tracts.

Bedford County includes the Smith Mountain Lake State Park, the Smith Mountain Lake Airport, The Virginia Dare Dinner Cruise, Mariner's Landing Resort and Conference Center, the Downtown Moneta development and much more. Bedford County Marinas include Camper's Paradise, Lake Haven Marina, Mitchell's Point Marina, Parkway Marina (formerly Saunders), Crystal Shores Marina Resort, Sportsman Inn Marina, Virginia Dare Marina, Moorman Marina, Halesford Harbour Marina, Smith Mountain Lake State Park Boat Rentals, Waterwheel Marina, Craddock Creek Marina, and Smith

Mountain Yacht Club. Local Bedford County stores include Food Lion, Diamond Hill Store (Devo's), White House Store, as well as the shops in the Downtown Moneta development, including the Celebration Square shopping center. There are a number of real estate offices on the Bedford County side of the lake including Long & Foster, Shoreline Realty, Realty World, and Lake Retreat Properties. Vacation rentals are handled by Bedford County agencies including CB Rentals, Lake Retreat Properties, Lakeshore Rentals and Mariner's Landing.

The growth of Bedford County has been greatly influenced in recent years by the vision of entrepreneurial developer George Aznavorian. Mr. Aznavorian was behind the completion of the Bedford County Wastewater Treatment System, which gave Bedford County commercial developments the ability to dramatically expand their sewage capacity. This allows for hotels, restaurants, higher-density development, and much more flexibility than is common in a rural county. He is also the driving force behind the Downtown Moneta development, the Mayberry Hills subdivision, and the drive-in theatre. Downtown Moneta, designed to have a Mayberry small town feeling, is the home of a variety of commercial and retail establishments as well as condominiums. The Bedford County/Smith Mountain Lake YMCA is located in downtown Moneta/Mayberry Hills.

Mariner's Landing is another waterfront resort in Bedford County. Developed by John and Matt White and company, this resort and conference center includes an 18-hole championship golf course designed by Robert Trent Jones, a conference facility, an excellent restaurant, a spa, three pools and a hot tub, a fitness center, and four miles of walking trails.

Bedford County also features the National D-Day Memorial, the Peaks of Otter, Thomas Jefferson's summer home (Poplar Forest), a number of vineyards, and a lovely section of the Blue Ridge Parkway. Bedford County has traditionally lagged behind Franklin County in commercial development and retail, but that has changed somewhat since the advent of the sewage system.

Section I: Introduction to Smith Mountain Lake

Bedford County boasts the closest direct views of Smith Mountain near the dam, and borders the widest and most popular part of the lake. Many people say Bedford County has more of a vacation feel than Franklin County. Much of the shoreline is dotted by cottages, chalets and cabins, though there are beautiful new homes as well. Many Bedford subdivisions were among the first developed at the lake. A number of residents along Sunset Point Drive claim to have the first lot sold on the lake or the first dock built. Given the vacation feel of the Bedford side of the lake, it is fitting that most vacation rental properties are here.

Bedford County has about 120 subdivisions on or around the waterfront. Some consist of a small, unknown group of old homes while others are nicely planned developments. Many mixed subdivisions have a blend of old and new, small and large, cottage and luxury homes. These subdivisions include Mountain View Shores, Beechwood West, Isle of Pines, Harbor Village, Valley Mills Crossing, Sunset Point, High Point, Beechwood Shores, Bass Cove, Year Round Shores, Saunders Point, Lynchburg Camp and many more. Other neighborhoods boast mostly newer and larger homes. These include Lakefield, The Reach, Longview Estates, Eastlake Pointe, Aspen Point, North Dam, Overlook Estates and The Waterways. There are a few very "woodsy" subdivisions such as Cedar Key and Gobbler's Ridge, and some vacation spots such as Silver Bay and Shangri La.

Franklin County

Franklin County's border runs along the southwestern shoreline of the Roanoke Channel. It also covers the entire northern shoreline of the Blackwater Channel as well as virtually the entire southern shore of the Blackwater. The Franklin County shoreline includes addresses in Hardy, Wirtz, Moneta, Glade Hill, Union Hall, and Penhook. Franklin County does not generally allow short-term vacation rentals, but there are some houses grandfathered under the old rules and there are many

The Definitive Guide to Smith Mountain Lake Real Estate

condos and townhomes that can be rented short-term. There are approximately 7,000 Franklin County waterfront property owners. Franklin County boasts the Smith Mountain Lake Community Park, the Westlake Shopping area, Bernard's Landing Resort & Conference Center, the Booker T. Washington National Monument, the Westlake Golf Course, the Waterfront Country Club and Bridgewater Plaza, as well as the prestigious Water's Edge Golf and Country Club Community. Franklin County also features the Blue Ridge Parkway, Blue Ridge Farm Institute, Ferrum College, and is a stop on *The Crooked Road*, Virginia's Appalachian Heritage Music Trail.

Franklin County Marinas include: All Seasons Marine Service, Bay Roc Marina, Bridgewater Marina and Boat Rentals, Crazy Horse Marina, Indian Pointe Marina, Magnum Point Marina, Lakeside Marina, Gill's Creek Marina and Lodge, Blue Ridge Campground and Marina, Pelican Point Yacht Club, Bayside Marina and Yacht Club, Blackwater Marina and Grill, Smith Mountain Dock and Lodge, Virginia Inland Sailing Association and Westlake Boat Rentals at Westlake Waterfront Inn.

Much of Franklin County has been the most convenient to shopping and businesses. Westlake Corner had the first major grocery store at the lake and many of the major businesses and other amenities have sprung up from the Westlake area to the Hales Ford Bridge. Westlake Towne Center and the surrounding development has the largest grocery store (Kroger), the Westlake Cinema, the first national furniture chain (Grand's Home Furnishings), and the first two major building supply stores at the lake (Capp's and Smith Mountain Building Supply). Westlake Towne Center also features banks, lighting and plumbing galleries, cabinet shops, interior designers, various gift shops, Curves, Wendy's and much more. There is an assisted living complex, Runk and Pratt, with 60 units and 36 independent living cottages.

The greater Westlake area includes The Lake Inn Motel, The Westlake Waterfront Inn, restaurants and shops, and

Section I: Introduction to Smith Mountain Lake

Virginia's largest Dairy Queen. RSI Rentals, and By The Lake Vacation Rentals, two of Smith Mountain Lake's premier vacation rental agencies, are in this area.

Long before the Westlake area boomed, commercial development was already under way at the Bridgewater area of Franklin County. This commercial center includes many retail and food venues. The Bridgewater Pointe Condo community is at the bridge as well. Additionally, there are a number of other boat rental venues near the bridge, including Parrot Cove Boat Rentals and Sales, which includes houseboat rentals. The many real estate offices near the bridge include Wainwright & Company REALTORS®, which houses the Smith Mountain Homes Team, ReMax Lakefront Realty, Century 21, Berkshire Hathaway Home Services, Advantage Realty, Assist-2-Sell, Lake and Land Realty, Realty World, Lake Team Realty, Lakewatch Realty, 1st Choice Realty and Weichert REALTORS®.

The role of visionary entrepreneur and developer Ron Willard in the development of Franklin County and Smith Mountain Lake as a whole cannot be overstated. Back in the early 1970's, when it was a mere power-generating reservoir with a shoreline dotted by trailers and cottages, Ron envisioned Smith Mountain Lake as a place that would one day attract visitors and retirees from around the nation. He persisted in his vision, and though it was decades in the making, his dream has become a reality. Ron and his Willard Companies are the developers and/or owners of The Boardwalk subdivision, The Farm subdivision, The Waterfront Country Club community, The Water's Edge Country Club community, and The Westlake Golf and Country Club. Ron is also the developer of Westlake Towne Center, the hub of commercial development at Smith Mountain Lake and the home of many businesses that serve the greater lake area (see above). Smith Mountain Lake's 20,000-plus residents, thousands of annual visitors, and hundreds of businesspeople owe Ron a great debt of gratitude for working tirelessly to make Smith Mountain Lake what it is today. Thanks Ron!

In contrast to Bedford County's vacation cottage feeling, Franklin County, for the most part, has more of a newer, residential feeling. Most of the newest developments at Smith Mountain Lake are in Franklin County. These subdivisions are dominated by larger new brick, stucco or Hardie-plank homes, though there are still a lot of cottages, chalets and condos as well. Many Franklin County residents are glad to be in a county where virtually no vacation rentals are allowed. Like much of the lake, Franklin County has wonderful views of Smith Mountain and the Blue Ridge Mountains.

There are more than 200 subdivisions on and near the water on the Franklin County side of the lake. There are wonderful developments with upscale homes including: Waverly, The Water's Edge, The Retreat, The Boardwalk, Park Place, Montego Bay, Southwind Key, Contentment Island, Boxwood Green, River Bay, Windtree, Virginia Key, The Waterfront, The Farm and many more. Like Bedford County, there are subdivisions where one can find a mix of old and new, large and small, vacation cottages and tract homes. These include Long Island Estates, Highland Lakes, Highland Shores, Fox Chase, Deer Creek Estates, Idlewood Shores, Hales Point, Pelican Point and Walnut Run.

Pittsylvania County

Pittsylvania is the third county that makes up the border of Smith Mountain Lake. Pittsylvania County comprises much of the far southeast corner of the lake and includes Smith Mountain itself as well as the dam. While this county has a small percentage of the residences at Smith Mountain Lake it has fantastic views and a few notable developments.

Pittsylvania County includes a mix of million dollar plus homes, older cottages, and trailers that are being displaced every year. The developments here are all on or near Smith Mountain Road, the main route through this area. This road leads north across a prominent peninsula to Vista Pointe Condos, one of the most prolific buildings on the lake. Vista

Section I: Introduction to Smith Mountain Lake

Pointe Condos feature amazing views of Smith Mountain to the east, the Roanoke Channel in three directions, and the Blackwater Channel to the west. This development includes a large swimming pool and sandy beach.

Pittsylvania County is home to Sanctuary Bay, one of the lake's up and coming subdivisions. Developed by the experienced team of Erik Plyler and company, this beautiful neighborhood includes 27 lots and nearly 100 planned upscale townhomes. Many of the views there are breathtaking. One home being built there is more than 10,000 square feet. In 2006, a lot there resold for more than $1.3 million, the third most expensive in the lake's history. The waterfront lots at Sanctuary Bay all sold out within weeks of being offered for sale, and the townhomes also promise to be a success.

The Smith Mountain Lake Dock and Lodge, Lumpkins Marina, the lovely Three Pointe Isle neighborhood, and the Visitor Center at Smith Mountain Dam are also in Pittsylvania County.

Recreation
In addition to its lovely terrain, friendly atmosphere and numerous amenities, Smith Mountain Lake is a recreation hotspot. Water sports abound, and there are numerous places to rent, buy, launch, dock and enjoy watercrafts of all types. Water skiers love Smith Mountain Lake for its long, wide runs and spacious glassy coves. Jet-skiers appreciate the room to move around and are often seen stealing the wakes of larger crafts to create a wild ride. Wake boarders love Smith Mountain Lake, too. Liquid Force, one of the world's premier wakeboard companies, hosted its first competition here. The company was so impressed that it hired photographers to shoot its catalogue shots here. (This was reportedly the first time Liquid Force™ has shot photos for its catalogue outside of Lake Powell in Arizona.) Parents have fun pulling their kids on kneeboards and tubes of all sizes and shapes, and families are regularly seen in canoes, kayaks and paddleboats. Some of the best photos shot at

The Definitive Guide to Smith Mountain Lake Real Estate

Smith Mountain Lake are of sailboats gliding across our crystal clear waters. Whatever type of boat you like can probably be found here at Smith Mountain Lake. Pontoon boats, deck boats, jet boats, rowboats, and even rowing sculls can be seen traversing our waters. Smith Mountain Lake was ranked third in the nation by USA Today as a best place to float a houseboat.

Fishing is another activity many of us enjoy. Well, at least some of us enjoy it – others are obsessed! It's easy to see why. Smith Mountain Lake has been recognized as one of the top fishing lakes in the United States according to various national publications and polls. ESPN did its first nationally televised fishing tournament here in June 2007. Top national fisherman loved it here, and it is reported that the national champion angler was looking for a vacation home here after the event. There are many outstanding charter guide-fishing services at Smith Mountain Lake, and their catches are impressive.

What impresses me more, however, is the way the average novice angler like me can enjoy landing a prize! My son, Jonathon, enjoyed the fight of his life landing a large fish right off our dock. Smith Mountain Lake is famous for Striper (striped bass), but it is also known for largemouth bass, smallmouth bass, crappie, bluegill (brim), and various types of catfish, carp, muskellunge and walleye. Smith Mountain Lake and the neighboring Leesville Lake hold records for two Virginia State freshwater catches. At least two striper bass of more than 50 pounds have been reportedly pulled from these waters.

Do you like to golf? Smith Mountain Lake has one of the top golf courses in America, according to Golf Digest Magazine. Michael Jordan and Shaquille O'Neal have been seen golfing there on more than one occasion. We enjoy five golf courses in our mountain community.

Do you like to hike? Smith Mountain Lake State Park has miles of beautiful hiking trails with numerous sightseeing vistas and bird watching opportunities. Smith Mountain Lake State Park is the jewel of Virginia's State Parks, which are ranked #1

Section I: Introduction to Smith Mountain Lake

among park systems in the United States. The State Park has a large beach and lodge as well as camping, boating and fishing facilities. Though not part of the State Park, visitors to the lake also enjoy the Smith Mountain Dam Visitor Center, which is open for tours 360 days a year.

Smith Mountain Lake offers many other recreational opportunities -- and the list is growing every year. I have listed an assortment of these activities in the section about "Amenities."

Just what is it about Smith Mountain Lake? What is drawing so many visitors, vacationers, and residents to our mountain lake? Why has it been deemed "The Crown Jewel of the Blue Ridge" and "Virginia's Best Kept Secret?" What drew actress Sissy Spacek here? Why does best-selling author David Baldacci live here at the lake? When filming "What About Bob?" with Bill Murray and Richard Dreyfuss here in 1991, why did the camera crews have to avoid shooting the breathtaking panoramic views of the mountains south of the lake? (Hint: They had to downgrade the shots to look like the more famous but less beautiful Lake Winnipesaukee in New Hampshire.) Why did HGTV's House Hunters choose Smith Mountain Lake over all of the lakes in the United States to shoot its waterfront special? Why did my client, then the Senior VP of Freddie Mac, pass over all the East Coast beach locations and the closer Lake Anna to purchase his weekend dream home here at Smith Mountain Lake? So many questions... one answer. You'll have to come and experience it yourself to find out.

If you've had the pleasure of spending much time here, you may agree with many others who say there's just no place like Smith Mountain Lake. I can't count the people I've met who say they've traveled the United States and have not found any place that provides the beauty and amenities that we enjoy here every day. For those of us who have relocated here, we can confidently say with Dorothy, "There's no place like home!"

How Do I Start My Lake Property Search?

The first step in your property search is to define what you are looking for. This will help you in your early conversations with a realty professional and save both of you time and headaches. The following is a list of questions you may want to consider before looking at specific property possibilities. If you are purchasing property with a spouse, children, other families or investment partners, it may be worth your time to review these issues together before proceeding.

I often counsel prospective buyers to break their search criteria into three sections. By putting answers to these questions in list form, it will help you move from the subjective to the objective and make your first discussions with a REALTOR® or early online searches more productive. We will touch on this again in more detail, but in summary:

(1) What could we accept at a minimum?
(2) What would our dream property look like?
(3) What would we never accept?

Below are specific issues you will want to consider before proceeding with your search. You may want to place the answers to the most important of these questions into the three categories above.

Purpose
Why are you doing this? What are your major goals?

Is this property primarily for recreational purposes?

Will this be your primary residence? Second or third home?
Is this property being purchased as an ongoing investment, to generate cash flow?

Section I: Introduction to Smith Mountain Lake

Are you buying this as a long-term investment, to gain equity? Are you buying this as a getaway to meet your kids who are going to Virginia Tech, Liberty University or University of Virginia? (This reason has been given by a number of my buyers in recent years!)

Are you planning to spend some weekends or a few weeks a year here? Do you plan to spend the summer here?

Do you plan to telecommute from here?

Do you plan to find a job locally?

How long do you plan to keep this property? If a long time, how could the slope of the lot and the steps impact you as you get older?

Do you plan to retire here? Will you trade or upgrade the property at that time?

Budget
What is the range that you are willing to spend on a home?

If you are buying a lot and plan to build, how well do you know your total costs upfront?

Have you factored the addition or expansion of a dock into the price of your building project?

Finance
How will you finance your purchase?

Do you need vacation rental income from the home to help finance your expenses?

Have you factored in property taxes, utilities, maintenance, and other costs associated with homeownership?

Will this property be part of a 1031 tax-deferred exchange?

How will tax write-offs from depreciation (if applicable), interest and other expenses assist you in the purchase?

How will leveraging your down payment through a mortgage affect your dollar-for-dollar return on investment?

Lot
Is a great view one of your top priorities? If so, what is a great view for you? Long water? Wide water? Sunsets? Sunrise? Mountains? View of grandkids jumping off a dock?

Is the steepness of the lot a factor? Will a large number of steps affect you or a loved one's enjoyment of the lake?

Do you want a large flat area for recreation?

Do you value trees and privacy?

Do you want a lot of acreage?

How will lot maintenance fit into your plans or expenses?

Dock and Waterfront
What type of dock do you need?

Do you need more than one boat slip?

Do you need deep water for the boat you have or plan to buy?

How many feet of waterfront do you want?

Section I: Introduction to Smith Mountain Lake

Do you prefer a beach, a riprapped shoreline, or some of both?

Do you prefer main channel or a cove property?

Home
What style of home do you prefer?

Do you want a log home?

Will you accept a doublewide?

Do you want a condo, townhome, patio home, or some other maintenance-free situation?

What age home do you prefer?

Are you willing to consider a fixer-upper or even a current or future teardown?

Neighborhood/Area
How close do you want to be to amenities such as a marina, shopping, fitness center or employment?

Do you mind living in an area with many vacation rentals nearby?

Do you prefer to live in a modern subdivision?

Do you desire to have…or want to avoid a strict property owners' association?

Do you want to live in a country club environment?

Is golf, tennis or a pool important to you?

I cannot emphasize enough the importance of interviewing and hiring a top-flight buyer's agent to assist you in your search. This is especially true due to the various issues that must be navigated to get you into your dream lake home. Buying a property here without the services of a REALTOR® is like going on trial without an attorney. I would never recommend this, but especially not here at a lake, which is likely not in your backyard and may have more potential pitfalls than a typical home in your subdivision. There are many full-time, experienced, honest and professional lake agents here who will gladly help you in your search. You may wish to start interviewing them right away.

Section II:
Assessing SML Property Values

What's in This Section?

How is Smith Mountain Lake Waterfront Property Valued? Seven Key Factors

What is the Quality of the Water at Smith Mountain Lake? Does Water Quality Affect Property Values?

How Does Water Depth Affect My Lake Experience and Property Value?

How Does The Rising and Falling Water Level Affect My Experience at Smith Mountain Lake?

Can I Dredge in Front of My Property to Get Deeper Water?

What is Riprap Anyway? What Options Do I Have to Control Erosion in Front of My Waterfront Property?

Can I Have a Dock? What about a Full Boathouse?

Can I Get a Beach?

Can I Cut Down or Trim Trees to Improve My View?

What Restrictions May I Face From Homeowner Associations?

What is a Water-Access Home?

How is Smith Mountain Lake Waterfront Property Valued? Seven Key Factors

Many people looking at home listings over the web are surprised when they see the wide variation in home prices here on the lake. They wonder why a beautiful, large waterfront home is priced hundreds of thousands lower than a run-down cottage in the same area. Or why some vacant lots are more expensive than nearby homes.

A number of factors contribute to property values here. As a result, values are not intuitively obvious, as they may be in a neighborhood in town. I have seen very costly mistakes on both sides of a transaction, and one of the main motivations for me to publish this guide is so that you won't overpay for a property.

One Note: In my opinion, it may not be enough to get a professional appraisal of a waterfront property you plan to buy or sell. Just last week I met with an owner whose property had just been appraised at $900,000 by a seemingly competent appraiser. Four realty agents he called independently valued the property around $700,000. The discrepancy was based on the fact that the appraiser's work was technical and "objective," while all of the agents also took into account the critical subjective issue that the home was right across the cove from a busy campground for RVs. The appraiser admitted he had not taken the marina into account. Another seller I met with told me how his home had recently been appraised for $800,000, yet it did not sell in six months on the market at $595,000. In my opinion, agents who work with home buyers daily often have a better grasp of actual market values on the street than many appraisers. Market value of a widely exposed property is based on the price that a willing buyer will pay and a willing seller will accept, which may be different from an appraiser's opinion.

Through interacting with many property owners, prospective buyers and actual buyers here on Smith Mountain Lake over the years, I have observed that there are seven major issues that affect the value of a waterfront home. Though there

Section II: Assessing SML Property Values

is obviously not a universal order, it seems that the following order is common for buyers of waterfront properties here.

Property Value Factor #1: View, View, View!

If you've been to the lake, you already know there are a marvelous variety of views here. Mountains, sunrises, sunsets, wildlife, wide-water and long-water views abound. There are properties that have virtually all of these components, but, as with anything in life, there are usually trade-offs. Whatever view is most valued by property buyers is *often* the #1 single issue that drove their purchase. Of course coveted views usually mean higher prices. While it is possible to enhance your view, as we will discuss in the section about tree removal and trimming, view is usually a factor that remains important regardless of what other factors are in play. "Location, Location, Location?" All Smith Mountain Lake properties have that. *The Lake itself is the location!* Here at the lake, we say "View, View, View!"

One quick note: There are a few waterfront properties here that have no view of the water from the home. Of course there are many off-water properties that have no view of the lake. If you can avoid these properties and get a home with a view, it will benefit the appreciation on your home as well as your enjoyment of the lake. If you can't afford a home with a view, you can still enjoy the lake from your boat most months of the year.

Property Value Factor #2: Slope

This factor often runs a close second behind view, and for many buyers it is first. Smith Mountain Lake's boundaries are made up of beautiful Blue Ridge Mountains that rise up from the water. Many waterfront lots are on old ridge tops or even peaks. Some of these lots are only 5 or 10 feet above the water level, which can result in nearly flat lots with a very gentle slope to the water. Some slopes are too small to even allow a walkout basement. A large number of lots have a gentle or medium slope to the water, and a home can be well situated with a nice view, a basement, and a reasonable driveway in front and walk to the water behind. There are other lots, however, that are steep. A few homeowners have actually added an electric tram to get from the house down to the water. Some homes require a golf cart or many steps.

Typically, the value of a waterfront property is directly affected by the slope. Once I showed a waterfront home with charm and privacy. It seemed like the perfect lake home, and the couple was very excited as they walked through it. That is, until they looked off the back deck. This was an unusually steep lot, and there were 105 steps down to the boathouse. They eventually walked down to the dock, and this confirmed that this was not the home for them (I *had* warned them before we went!).

Often, you will be able to get a nicer home in a nicer area with a better view if you are willing to sacrifice on the slope. And who knows – you may be able to stay in great shape by doing the stairs!

Property Value Factor #3: Waterfront
What does "waterfront" mean in this context? This is a catch-all phrase, I admit. This issue is often third on folks' lists, but is sometimes first or second. Factors may include:

- **Length of Shoreline**. Though many buyers dream of having a great deal of shoreline for privacy and recreation, I often find that most owners use only a small area anyway. A typical lot here at the lake has about 100 feet of shoreline. Note that if there is not a dock on the property, you will need to be sure that there is enough shoreline (and that the property line angles are right if you are in the back of a tight cove) to construct the dock you desire.
- **Water Depth**. Most buyers want deep water off the end of their dock. This provides a great opportunity to launch your boat, the depth needed to jump from the top of the

Section II: Assessing SML Property Values

boathouse (my kids love this!), and the depth in the unlikely event of a large drop in the lake level. While deep water is nice, and it is common here, I have seen many homes with only a few feet of water that have worked out fine for the most part. Note that it is often (but not always) the case that deep water and a gently sloping lot conflict with one another since the slope of the land usually continues out into the lake. Also note that there are some advantages to having shallower water, especially for a swimming area for younger children. My ideal waterfront lot is shallow at the edge then drops off where the dock will be.

- **Water Quality.** This is not a big issue here in general, since the water is outstanding throughout most of the lake. There are a few places that have murky water from time to time, especially after winter and spring rains. Conversely, there are also some places on the lake that are known for having especially crystal clear water regardless of the weather or other factors. The former case, since it is the exception, has more effect on price than the latter.
- **Beach.** Beaches are uncommon here, but owners and their children enjoy them. A thorough MLS search can often turn up properties with a beach if this is important to you. Ask your agent to do this search for you.
- **Erosion Control at Shoreline.** Most properties at the lake use riprap erosion control. These are rocks, fist-sized or larger, that are put above the water level and down into the water to hold back the shore and prevent erosion. This can be done attractively and can enhance the value of a waterfront lot. This should generally not be done on flat areas that do not experience much erosion.
- **Dock.** The quality, style, size and general appearance of a dock can certainly impact the value of the property. Though docks are important, they can usually be altered or replaced. I haven't seen docks as a critical driver or deterrent in the price of a home or lot in *most* cases.

The Definitive Guide to Smith Mountain Lake Real Estate

Property Value Issue #4: The Home
If the property has a house, and it is a house that the buyers intend to keep and/or remodel, this is often #4 on the list. Most buyers here are already risk-takers. Many own businesses and/or have built or substantially remodeled homes and see that the previously mentioned items (view, slope, waterfront) are more permanent in nature, while the home can be remodeled, added onto, or bulldozed. This explains why I am showing a lot with a single-wide trailer on it next week priced at $1 million, and am showing lovely new homes to others for half that price.

Property Value Factor #5: Location, Location, Location
This issue is way down the list here at Smith Mountain Lake because location is already established. Everyone choosing to buy at Virginia's Jewel of the Blue Ridge already has THE location, wherever they are on the lake! So the specific area of the lake is typically less important in the valuation of the home.

That being said, there are still various reasons why owners may want to be in a certain part of the lake or in a particular subdivision. For example, buyers who want to live in a private country club community with one of the top golf courses on the East Coast would want to buy a home at The Water's Edge. Buyers looking for upscale homes in a private wooded community may choose Waverly, among many others. A buyer looking for a Nantucket style home that gives a feeling of being at the beach may look at The Boardwalk. Someone wanting to sail may try to be near the Pelican Point Yacht Club. Others may want a more rural feel, a subdivision feel, be close to certain amenities, be in an area of many rentals, or be away from rentals.

Driving time is also an issue. However, buyers often find that this is less important once they truly time the drive from home to various parts of the lake. It seems the spots that appear least convenient have the straightest access roads, so the actual drive times are similar from many locations to most lake destinations. For example, it is about the same drive time from

Section II: Assessing SML Property Values

the south (say from Raleigh, North Carolina) to parts of Huddleston, in the northeast corner of the lake, as it is to parts of Union Hall, in the southern part of the lake. One would not guess this when looking at a map. Similarly, it is about the same time to drive from north of the lake (say from Roanoke) to both Huddleston and Union Hall. In fact the drive time from D.C. to many parts of the lake is about the same, though one would not guess this from a map. As George Clooney said, "Well isn't that just a geographical oddity!"

The issue of a property's location on the channels may also come up. Some buyers prefer to be right in the middle of the action, say in the area of Smith Mountain Lake State Park on the main channel. Others don't care about wide water and would rather be in a private location way up the Blackwater or Roanoke Channels. All else being equal, home values are *often* higher in a more central part of the lake.

Another issue is the proximity to shopping and other services. When the Westlake Corner area of the lake, in Franklin County, was one of the few with shopping and other commercial services, that area experienced booming growth. Now that a public sewage system is installed in Bedford County and the south side of the lake is getting more retail and commercial development as well, this is not as much of an issue.

Property Value Factor #6: Cove versus Main Channel
This issue is not completely cut and dry because there are varying degrees of land in coves, on the main channel, and in between. Many first-timers here at the lake assume that they will want to be on the main channel, which often provides the longest and widest water and mountain views. Most, but certainly not all, experienced homeowners and renters here seem to prefer to be in a cove, however, at least to some degree. Cove homes typically provide more solitude, less boat noise, and a better spot for swimming. A great spot for both views and solitude can be near the edge of a cove with views out to wide

water. There are countless spots like this on the lake. One note: There are homes positioned in coves in such a way as to greatly limit their views and water quality. These are properties that you want to avoid if possible.

Both cove and main channel homes have great value and opportunity for appreciation. You just need to decide what is best for you and your family.

Property Value Factor #7: Lot Size
We often get first inquiries from people asking for the typical price of property per acre here. While there are rare individuals who really want more acreage, most buyers value the factors discussed above so much more that the size of the lot really doesn't matter. Exceptions are a lot so small that it is unworkable, or a prime lot with a great view and slope in a great part of the lake that *also* has a few acres. This could be a great benefit for some.

As evidence of what I am saying, my waterfront lots site (**SmithMountainHomes.com/Listing-Lots**) at one time had two correctly priced lots to consider. One was a 46-acre tract with more than a half-mile of shoreline priced at $612,000. A second lot had about 1.4 acres with 811 feet of shoreline and was priced at $1.375 million. Both sold near these prices.

As another example, a number of years back I sold a waterfront lot with more than five acres and 300 feet of shoreline for $210,000. In the same month I sold a 1.5-acre waterfront lot, also with over 300 feet of shoreline, for $825,000. In both these situations, the higher priority factors listed above drove the price, both to the high and low sides.

There may be specific situations in which acreage is a big plus, as for a developer for example. However acreage is not usually a high priority when looking for a waterfront home.

Section II: Assessing SML Property Values

What is the Quality of the Water at Smith Mountain Lake? Does Water Quality Affect Property Values?

Excellent water quality is one reason people are flocking to Smith Mountain Lake. The vast majority of spots on more than 500 miles of shoreline have crystal clear water year-round.

Unfortunately, as in any fresh body of water, a few places have less than perfect water quality in certain seasons of the year. These are typically right at the mouth of a few small stream inlets in the back of certain coves.

This poses a potential problem for buyers visiting the lake during the 90% of days during which the water in front of these homes is clear. You may visit and find that the price on a lot or home seems lower than other similar properties. Without a realty agent who is *both knowledgeable and honest*, you may find yourself purchasing a property with less than perfect year-round water quality. You may get an honest agent who is not aware of the water quality variations in a particular cove or near a certain inlet – but that won't help you. Or you can imagine the scores of problems that could result from retaining a less than honest agent whose desire for a commission is stronger than their desire to serve you. It is unlikely this will be a problem for you here at Smith Mountain Lake.

Your enjoyment of the lake will not usually be affected much at most properties with water quality variations. The water will typically be clear for most of time you are enjoying the lake. It will often, however, affect the value and appreciation of your home, as well as the time on the market when you choose to sell. You may even want to purchase a nicer home in an area with less than perfect water quality. This may save you money and suit you just fine.

How Does Water Depth Affect My Lake Experience and Property Value?

The depth of water in front of your home will affect both the value and long-term enjoyment of your home. While a few buyers are looking for shallow water to launch a certain type of craft or for children's play off the shore, most are seeking deep water. Though deep water is a comfort, most boat owners discover that they can launch virtually any boat from most properties at Smith Mountain Lake. I once built and sold a home in a shallow cove with normal water depths in the two- to three-foot range. The neighbor owned a medium-sized sailboat (with a much deeper hull than most power boats) that he docked there and seemed to have no trouble getting in and out. Since I show properties by boat, I regularly go in and out of many of the shallower coves on the lake and I can't recall having a problem docking my boat. (One reason this is not a problem here is the general stability of the water level. Virtually all properties have fixed docks and even on rare occasions when the water level does drop, it doesn't significantly affect boating.)

Section II: Assessing SML Property Values

How Does the Rising and Falling Water Level Affect my Experience at Smith Mountain Lake?

Many people who visit Smith Mountain Lake are surprised that the water levels do not fluctuate much. Other man-made lakes controlled by power companies see significant, regular fluctuations. Lake Norman, in North Carolina, fluctuates so much that, in some cases, docks have to be built on a pivoting mechanism more than 100 ft. from shore. Homeowners there say they are often looking at a mud bowl in the winter rather than a beautiful lake. The long piers and docks are sometimes sitting in mud, and their boats are sitting in storage.

In the winter of 2007, many of us were seeing pictures in the news of Lake Lanier, near Atlanta, which had become a virtual dried up mud hole with grass growing hundreds of feet out from the normal shoreline. There were reports that Atlanta would soon lose its water supply if rain didn't come soon. Five million people there held their breath to see what would happen.

Due in part to the outstanding design of the Smith Mountain Lake hydroelectric system, we enjoy relatively stable water levels. In fact, most boathouses are built close to shore and don't require a swivel mechanism for fluctuating lake levels. To my knowledge, water levels have never dropped to a level in which the enjoyment and functionality of the lake is significantly impacted for most people.

Note that our neighbor, Leesville Lake, offers properties at significantly lower prices than Smith Mountain Lake. Leesville Lake, however, experiences fluctuation in water levels – up to six feet above or below normal lake level. If you want to save money and don't mind this fluctuation, we can show you around Leesville Lake as well.

Can I Dredge in Front of my Property to Get Deeper Water?

What about dredging? Will you be able to dredge the area at your shoreline and in front of your dock? Well, often, but not always. There are rules that determine which properties can be dredged and which cannot. Although it may seem counter-intuitive, some of the shallowest areas are those that cannot be dredged. If the lake bottom near your lot is between 793 and 795 above sea level (this translates to up to about two feet deep or less), dredging will likely not be permitted. If the water is deeper than about two feet at full pond, then dredging of accumulated sediment (not the natural lake bottom) may be allowed. Dredging must occur outside of the fish-spawning period of March 1 through June 30. Though the governing body that oversees this is certainly not fanatically pro-environment and anti-development, these rules must be followed for the good of fish spawning and hatching within the lake, and thus for the future of the lake and all of us who enjoy it.

Some buyers assume they will be able to dredge and are later disappointed. If this is a concern for you, you may contact the Army Corps of Engineers in Christiansburg, Virginia, which issues the permits and can explain how it works. You can reach the Army Corps at (540) 382-6740. The AEP Shoreline Management Plan (see **smithmtn.com**) explains these rules in more detail. If water depth is a concern for you, you may even wish to make your offer contingent on obtaining approval to dredge your shoreline.

By the way, one strategy for obtaining a great deal is to buy a home that has a price abnormally discounted due to shallow water depth and then have the property dredged. I had a buyer who did this. Often the cost of dredging will be far less than the savings you achieve because other buyers didn't take the effort to investigate this.

Section II: Assessing SML Property Values

What about you? Are you looking for shallow water? Do you need deep water? Be sure to ask your realty agent to help you find out the depth of the water in front of the property you are interested in. Find out if you will ever be able to dredge, if this is a concern. If you are touring property by boat, some of this should be discovered before you even reach the property.

What is Riprap Anyway? What Options Do I Have to Control Erosion in Front of my Waterfront Property?

The rocks placed along a shoreline to control erosion are referred to as riprap (not riff-raff!). Is a riprapped shoreline something you want or not? If the property you want does not have this, can you get it? Well, it depends.

A riprapped versus a grassy shoreline is really a matter of preference. Generally, if you have a steep, sharply cut bank at the shoreline, you will want to have riprap as protection against erosion. The majority of developed lots and homes already have this in place if it is needed. If it should have been in place but is not, there are measures that can be taken. Check the Shoreline Management Plan for more information.

Can you automatically have riprap installed on your shoreline where you wish? No, you cannot. The Power Company that manages Smith Mountain Lake has rules that determine what part of shoreline can and cannot have erosion control. Generally speaking, a property that has evidence of current erosion will be eligible for riprap. If your property has a beach, wetlands, or a very consistent gentle slope from the land into the water, however, it is often not a good candidate for erosion control. Most people who have a beach or this type of shoreline, however, want to keep it this way and wouldn't want riprap anyway.

The rule is that your lot likely qualifies as a riprap candidate if there is "active erosion." Active erosion is defined by the Shoreline Management Plan as 1) areas that are bare and void of vegetation or other stabilizing material, 2) areas that are experiencing undercuts and/or sloughing off of the parent material, or 3) areas directly adjacent to the shoreline that have the potential to deposit sediment or soil material into the lake. This can be true whether the lot is flat or steep. It partially depends on the currents and boat traffic in the area of the lot.

Section II: Assessing SML Property Values

If you have a property that is experiencing erosion, it is critical to deal with it. I know of one beautiful, nearly flat point lot owned by some wonderful folks from another area. Because they did not take the simple and relatively inexpensive measures necessary to control erosion, their lot has shrunk 10% to 20% in size. Don't let this happen to you.

Can I Have a Dock? What About a Full Boathouse?

This is an important question. There are some lakes that, for one reason or another, do not allow the wonderful types of docks that we enjoy here at Smith Mountain Lake. Some lakes have such a large variation in water levels that stationary boathouses are not possible. Other lakes have such strict environmental and building code regulations that a nice boathouse is not allowable. Some lakes are in hurricane belts, and therefore do not allow indoor structures that may be more susceptible to being damaged and to cause damage to other properties in high winds.

Smith Mountain Lake is blessed with a wide assortment of boathouse and dock styles and sizes. However, in the past several years limitations have been placed on the construction of new docks. It used to be that waterfront property owners could build just about any type and size of dock they wished. They could even build living quarters above their boat slip (there are still a few of these around the lake now). As the lake has become so popular, the rules for dock size, style and placement needed to change. In 2003, the definitive Shoreline Management Plan was issued by Appalachian Power (American Electric Power or AEP) in conjunction with The Federal Energy Regulatory Commission (FERC). This plan defines guidelines for docks, erosion control, beaches, home sites and much more. The following sections highlight some of the regulations covered under Shoreline Management.

Allowance for a Dock

Appalachian Power wants people to have a dock for their property. However, it is critical that the dock not hamper anyone else's enjoyment of the lake. Therefore, to install, expand, or significantly refurbish a dock on your property, you must apply for a permit. This is inexpensive and not overly complicated, but it is important that it be done correctly. This permit will require that you draw the dock on a plat of your lot, showing the dimensions, style and other information. Ask a

Section II: Assessing SML Property Values

realty agent if they are willing to assist you in filing a dock permit, or call AEP at (540) 489-2556.

Lots subdivided before the Shoreline Management Plan went into effect in 2003 can *generally* obtain a dock permit. However, lots developed after the Plan generally need to have at least 100 feet of shoreline to obtain a dock permit unless a dock easement was provided at some point. (There is a rumor that all lots must have 100 feet of shoreline to build a dock, but this is not the case – it is generally only lots developed after the Plan went into effect. Most lots allow for a dock since developers generally make sure new lots meet this requirement.)

If you're buying a lot or a home without a dock, it is critical that you personally check the length of the shoreline to verify what is reported in the realty listing. If there is less than 100 feet, you should also have your agent verify the year the lot was subdivided. Note that it is not always obvious where to measure the shoreline. For example, I once sold a point lot that had about 200 feet of shoreline reported on the plat at the 800-foot contour line. The actual shoreline, however, is at the 795-foot contour line, and the shoreline there exceeded 300 feet. This was a wonderful benefit to the owners, but can work against you as well. Some of the regulations pertain to the shoreline at the actual lake level of 795 feet above sea level; others pertain to 800 feet above sea level. AEP regulates up to the 800-foot contour line.

Dock Setbacks

In order to assure that enjoyment of the lake is not hampered, new docks must be positioned at least 15 feet inside the property line and at least 30 feet from any other structure (e.g. the neighbor's dock).

If the dock is in a cove, and you are not the last dock in the back of that cove, the dock must not extend across more than one-third of the cove. This rule provides for one-third of the cove on each side to be utilized by docks, and leaves one-third in the middle for boats to pass through. If your property is in the back of the cove, and your dock would not encroach on neighbors' boating, it is possible in some cases to have the standard setbacks as well as the rules regarding the width of the dock across the cove waived. This may require obtaining permission from neighbors. Most coves on Smith Mountain Lake are not that narrow, so this rule does not often come into play.

Dock Size and Style

Boathouses and docks cannot be completely enclosed, but a 72 square foot enclosed room can still be built within the structure of a dock. (This is reportedly better than other lakes, including some in North Carolina, which have completely prohibited any interior rooms on docks.)

In general, eligible waterfront properties with up to 300 feet of shoreline can have one or more docks totaling 1,500 square feet. These docks can have up to two full covered boat slips and any number of personal watercraft spaces. The dock may include additional covered areas, a stationary dock area, and floating docks. Additional boats can be docked at the stationary and floating dock areas.

Properties with 301 feet to 600 feet of shoreline are eligible for a three covered slip boathouse with up to 2,250 square feet. It is possible for these lots to have multiple docks totaling 2,250 square feet.

Properties with 601 feet to 900 feet of shoreline are eligible for a four covered slip boathouse with up to 3,000 square feet. It is possible for these lots to have multiple docks totaling 3,000 square feet.

For each 300 feet of linear shoreline, an additional 750 square feet and one boat slip can be added to the total dock area. Note that the maximum size of a single structure can be 3,000 square feet with a minimum of 30 feet between structures. Construction of three or more total slips requires an adjacent residence with functioning restroom facilities.

Section II: Assessing SML Property Values

Some people think you can have only one dock on your property with up to 1,500 or 2,250 square feet, etc. per the shoreline footage. Actually, the Shoreline Management Plan allows for multiple docks totaling this square footage on most properties. The Shoreline Management Plan provides more details on these regulations.

Also note that the square footage limits do not generally include the walkways out to the dock. The limits do, however, include the "aerial view" square footage of the dock, so roof overhangs or other peripheral structures that exceed the boundaries of the dock floor may be counted in the total.

Structures located between the 800-foot contour and the lake (above 795-foot contour) are limited to a structure that provides access to the dock. This includes a stairway, ramp or landing that connects the dock to the land. The maximum width of this structure is six feet. Floating walkways can be eight feet in width.

Grandfathered Docks
Since the Shoreline Management Plan was issued, AEP realized there would be situations in which docks that were damaged or destroyed would need to be rebuilt. In the event of a fire or other problem, would property owners be allowed to rebuild docks as they were, even if they did not conform to the current regulations regarding size, style or placement?

Over a decade ago, the Power Company established a deadline of August 2005, giving property owners with non-conforming docks several months to submit applications and detailed drawings and photos of their docks. The issues that defined the non-conformance included the size, setbacks, and style of docks. These forms were not always immediately reviewed in detail, but were filed for future eventualities such as damage or destruction of a dock.

Should the non-conforming dock issue matter to you? Absolutely! If you buy a home here with a non-conforming dock, you will want to be sure that you can rebuild the same or better dock in the same or better location. It is important that you or your agent understand the rules and know who to contact to see if the non-conforming documents are on file.

As an example, I was recently part of a transaction that went south due to the non-conforming dock issue. The dock was built in the very back of a cove, which was OK, but only one foot from the neighbor's property line (the dock was built prior to the rule change). Unfortunately, the seller had not bothered to file the application for the non-conforming dock. The astute purchaser, upon viewing the plat and being well advised by the realty agent, asked for a copy of the non-conforming paperwork. When it was not available, and other efforts were undertaken and failed, the purchaser walked away.

By the way, if a non-conforming permit is not on file, there are several other options available to solve a non-conforming dock situation. One common option is to proactively seek an easement from a neighbor to allow a dock to be rebuilt at the same spot where it exists currently (in the event that the current structure is destroyed or significantly damaged in the future).

Since the dock is critical for most waterfront property buyers, this is too important to ignore. A quick overview of the Shoreline Management Plan first will help you in this process.

Finding the Right Dock Builder
Not all dock builders are created equal. Not all dock builders treat their clients fairly. Not all finish their work on time, build the dock they promise, or bother to check and adhere to the subdivision and power company rules before installing a dock or boathouse. Not all docks cost the same. On the other hand, there are many great dock builders here at Smith Mountain Lake. Be sure to get personal recommendations and references for any dock builder before signing a contract.

Floating Docks on Long Piers vs. Boathouses at the Shore
Some visitors to Smith Mountain Lake are pleasantly surprised to find that the docks here are usually much more than simple

Section II: Assessing SML Property Values

floating platforms at the end of long piers. Most are semi-enclosed structures with roofs, indoor rooms, and electric hoists that suspend boats above the water. We are proud to inform visitors that the ability to have these docks is due to the stability of the water level here. In general, the water levels here fluctuate so little that a permanent dock with a floating component works perfectly. This also allows owners to keep their boats onsite year 'round rather than pay a marina to store their boats in the off-season. I have been able to take my boat out on the lake in mid-winter on numerous occasions as well.

As mentioned elsewhere, other lakes experience significant level fluctuations that make a simple floater the best option for docking their boats. Unless a special air suspension hoist is installed, this can result in wear on the boat from leaving it in the water as well as the slime (a technical term for "gunk") that accumulates on the bottom of the boat. Significant additional wear results from the constant sunlight the boat receives at a dock like this -- and this is not as easily correctable. Another troubling effect from the fluctuating levels at other lakes is the appearance and functionality of the shoreline when levels are down. A friend at Lake Norman tells me that it is an ugly sight to see his floating dock sitting in 100 feet of mud. Property owners here have truly been blessed with a beautiful situation in regard to stable lake levels, docks, views, and much, much more. I thank God for the opportunity to be here at Smith Mountain Lake!

Can I Get a Beach?

What about a beach? Are there natural beaches on the lake? Can I install a beach?

Many people want a beach on their Smith Mountain Lake shoreline. There are many naturally occurring beaches at the lake, and I have owned several lots here with nice beaches. These are great places to walk into the water or to let kids play by the shoreline. Though they are available, most buyers don't know that there is a systematic way to locate these homes and lots on the lake rather than just looking at many properties and hoping to find one with an existing beach.

For example, I had clients from Washington, D.C., who planned to find a waterfront lot to build their dream home. They had young children, and after two trips to the lake, decided they really had to have a lot with a beach. The next morning, we went by boat to the seven waterfront lots in their price range with a beach. After going back to their top three by car, they chose one and were the owners within several weeks.

If you want a beach, don't waste weeks visiting properties all over the lake, hoping to find one. Make use of the technology available to find it online first.

By the way, can you construct a beach on a lot where there is not one? Generally, it is not allowed and is not a good idea anyway. However, I have a man-made beach at my home, and you should be able to build one as well – above the 800-foot contour. There are disadvantages to building a new beach like this, however, so it is ideal if you can find a property with an existing man-made or natural beach.

Section II: *Assessing SML Property Values*

Can I Cut Down or Trim Trees to Improve my View?

Many clients ask if they will be able to remove or trim trees on their lot to enhance their view of the lake and mountains and enhance the beauty of their yard and landscaping. Some buyers come from areas with stricter regulations on cutting trees and altering native plants. The good news is that yes, in general, you can control your view.

First of all, there are no significant regulations on the removal of trees and other plants throughout your property *above* the 800-foot contour (on most of the lot). (As a quick reminder, the normal lake level, referred to here as "full pond," is 795 feet above sea level.) AEP regulates the shoreline up to the 800-foot level, which is five feet vertically above the lake. This often translates to about 6 to 15 feet (or much more on a flatter lot) from the shore, depending on the slope of the lot. The area below the 800-foot contour is referred to by AEP as the "Project Boundary."

Clearing Your Lot Outside of the Project Boundary
If you purchase a wooded lot and wish to clear it for a home site or just to enhance its value above the 800-foot contour, you will need to apply for a permit from the county planning and zoning office. This E&S (Erosion and Sediment control) permit ensures that proper measures are undertaken with regard to erosion control. It also ensures that sediment will not be dumped into the lake, which protects other property owners and the beauty and usability of the lake as a whole. Any good excavation contractor should be able to apply for this permit for you and will know how to take steps to ensure compliance. (Usual compliance consists of erecting and maintaining a simple silt fence.) One great aspect of this E&S permit is the simplicity by which it is obtained. Like other permits here in our rural counties, there is no significant waiting time, hassle or expense involved. As in the acquisition of a building permit, it is

typically a matter of filling out a simple application, paying a small fee, and posting a sign on your lot. Again, I am referring to a full scale clearing of your lot, not the simple removal or trimming of trees, so this E&S permit is worst-case scenario for the area above the 800-foot contour.

Removal and Trimming of Trees Outside Project Boundary
There is typically no regulation that will prohibit you from removing or trimming individual trees in your yard (still above the 800-foot contour). Most waterfront homeowners remove trees to open up their view. A good lake landscaper can also recommend ways to artfully trim trees to enhance the view and enjoyment of your lot.

There are certain lake subdivisions, such as Waverly, which regulate the removal and significant trimming of trees on owners' property. To keep a more natural, woodsy look, the property owners' association committee reviews a simple application for major tree and landscaping work. If you have driven through Waverly, by the way, you will see that they have done an exceptional job in this regard. Many wish that more subdivisions would adopt these types of restrictions.

Trimming and Removal of Trees within Project Boundary
If you desire to significantly trim or remove trees between the 800-foot contour and the lake, in the area managed by the power company, a bit more effort is involved. The power company's goal is to protect the shoreline from erosion and prevent sediment from dropping into the lake. The root systems of trees and other foliage is an excellent soil stabilizer, so to remove them extensively may have a negative impact on your lot, your shoreline area, and the lake in general.

To remove trees from this area, you will need to apply for a permit from Appalachian Power Company. In general, AEP will allow you to remove any trees or plants that are dead, damaged, or smaller than one-half inch in diameter at breast height. You are also permitted to completely clear all trees and other foliage

Section II: Assessing SML Property Values

in a six-foot continuous section for your dock. Additionally, regulations provide the opportunity for removing trees *on a case-by-case basis* without replacing them for the benefit of view. The rule of thumb for opening up this view-shed is to allow complete clearing of about 10% of the width of the lot at the shoreline. This would generally be allowable at a more densely treed lot as compared with one that already has a "reasonable view." (Note that it is *critical* that you check these facts with AEP and run your specific situation by their personnel. Though I believe what I am quoting per the Shoreline Management Plan, I have heard of situations where these rules seemed to be enforced differently.)

Other trees along the shoreline can be removed, but most often they must be replaced with native plants of the same total collective size. For example, if you remove a total of 75 inches in diameter of trees at the shoreline, you will need to purchase and replant 75 inches in other native plants in the same area (except for the area allowed to open up the view). The benefit of this approach is the replacement of tall, view-blocking trees with short, attractive native plants that don't block the view, that enhance the landscaping, and that still possess the root systems necessary to control erosion. The Shoreline Management Plan will provide you with a list of eligible native plants. Many local landscapers are familiar with this process.

Another approach is to keep the shoreline area trees in place and trim them to open up the view. There are no significant regulations on trimming trees within the Project Boundary. The Plan recommends, but does not regulate, that trees not be trimmed too severely. As long as the root systems are kept in place (which trimming should not usually affect), the trimming is left up to you. I know landscapers who can trim a tree way up the trunk and make this look beautiful and effectively open the view. As you traverse the lake, notice how other properties have been landscaped, and how trees have been extensively trimmed at lower levels. You don't need to receive a permit to trim trees at the shoreline.

Note that for both the county erosion and sediment control permit and the AEP permit, officials may come out and inspect your property before, during and after the work is done, so be careful to create a good plan and stick to it.

Cutting Down Your *Neighbor's* Trees for Fun and Profit!
So you've found that perfect property, a vacation or retirement home that has a beautiful lot, a cozy home, and the perfect shoreline. But there's one problem: A key part of your view is blocked by the neighbor's trees. Is there anything that can be done? Well... maybe.

Don't be shy. Feel free to contact the neighbor and ask if he or she will consider cutting down or trimming certain trees. You want to make friends with your neighbor anyway, right? This will be a chance to meet and begin to build a relationship. You may even want to take this step before purchasing your property. You may find that the neighbor wanted to remove or trim those trees anyway, so it could be a win-win situation.

Typically, you will want to plan to offer to pay for the tree work done on your neighbor's property. It may be appropriate for you to procure bids from contractors and help to oversee and interact with them as well. Often you may be able to get a contractor to add the tree work at your neighbor's property to work you already have planned for your lot, sometimes decreasing the incremental cost next door.

This really works sometimes. A client of ours from New Jersey who had just contracted to purchase a waterfront weekend home here remarked how great his future view *would be* if the neighbor's trees were trimmed or removed. We checked the county tax records for the owner's name, and found his number online. We contacted the neighbor and met with him to review which trees we were requesting to be cut down or trimmed. He agreed to do so at our client's expense, and the work was done within days after closing.

This story has a great sidebar. When his view was opened up, we were all thrilled to see that his home now had a coveted

Section II: Assessing SML Property Values

straight-on view of Smith Mountain. Now he was able to enjoy the view from the home far more than he expected when he purchased it. This caused an immediate increase in the value of his home as well. (If the previous owner had thought of this, the purchase price on the home would have been quite a bit higher.)

A year-and-a-half later, our client loved Smith Mountain Lake so much that he sold his company in New Jersey and moved here full-time. When he went to sell his first lake home to upgrade to a full-time home, the exquisite view added to his sale price and decreased the time on the market.

One warning: Be sure the neighbors *clearly* mark every tree and every branch they are willing to have removed or trimmed. Ideally, your neighbor should be there on-site when the contractor is doing the work on his lot. You don't want to be blamed for tree removal that was never permitted by the neighbor. A waterfront homeowner here told me of a situation where a neighbor paid for his trees to be removed and the contractor cut down two trees that he had not agreed to. Since this benefited the other party, he was suspicious that the man who paid the bill was behind this action, and it strained the relationship between the neighbors from that time on.

What Restrictions May I Face From Homeowner Associations?

Many buyers come to Smith Mountain Lake to get away from suburbia. They want to escape tract homes, small lots, crowded cul-de-sacs and subdivision rules. These buyers are likely to purchase a home in a subdivision without significant covenants and restrictions. Other buyers want to ensure that the value of their home will not be damaged by an oddball house built nearby. They may choose a subdivision with more restrictions. Fortunately, Smith Mountain Lake offers both options, and many in between. We have a number of subdivisions that strictly enforce the architecture, placement, size, and even exterior colors of the homes in their development. A few even require an application to cut down trees. There are other places on the lake, however, that allow cottages, strange homes, and even an occasional doublewide. Home values in both types of areas have appreciated at an excellent rate.

It is important for you, as a home buyer, to review the covenants and restrictions, if any, for the property you are considering. If you plan to build a log home, for example, it is important to ask a REALTOR® to show you only lots in neighborhoods that allow for the construction of these homes.

If you plan to stay in a Winnebago or some type of travel trailer before your home is complete, you need to check with the neighborhood homeowners' association, as well as the county, to see what rules may apply.

Some waterfront home buyers *really* want it all. Not only do they want a pristine mountain, sunsets over the lake, and a beautiful home – they also want horses and other farm animals! Amazingly, there are still some rural parts of the lake where this is possible. A number of years back I helped market a 40+ acre parcel that would have been perfect for this.

Section II: *Assessing SML Property Values*

What is a Water-Access Property?

Perhaps you are convinced that you want to live at our mountain-lake paradise, but being on the waterfront is not a priority. Maybe you would rather have a nicer home at a better price-point. Or perhaps you want to live near the lake yet have a place to launch your boat or to dock it. If this is you, a water-access home may be the ticket.

A buyer from out of the area called the other day hoping that water-access referred to waterways or canals that were cut into neighborhoods from the lake, as in Florida or other areas. I had to inform them that it is just not that good – nor as expensive. Water-access properties generally refer to homes or lots that have deeded access to a boat launch ramp or even a deeded dock. There are many waterfront subdivisions around the lake that have this type of property available. These lots and homes are usually available at a significant discount under the price of a waterfront home or waterfront lot nearby. Another classification of property is "off-water", which is a generic term for properties near the lake without deeded access. These properties still benefit from the opportunity to rent a boat slip nearby or launch a boat at a marina or park for a small fee.

Sometimes buyers are able to purchase a very nice water-access property for less than they could buy a similar lot or home for in a subdivision in a suburb of a larger city. For example, a number of years back there was a nice water-access lot with a limited view of the lake for sale in Beechwood West for $34,000. This lot, or a water-access home there, would provide owners all the benefits of the subdivision including a boat launch, two picnic areas, a racquetball facility, a basketball court, a workout room, a boat storage lot, tennis courts and more. If you want to live at Smith Mountain Lake without the cost of a waterfront home, a water-access property, condominium, or townhome may be the way to go.

Section III:
SML Investment Properties

What's in This Section?

I Want to Rent Out My Home. Are All SML Homes Rentable?

How Do I Find the Perfect Rental Home?

Is There Cash Flow Potential from a Waterfront Rental Home?

I Want to Rent Out my Home. Are All SML Homes Rentable?

Many home buyers here at Smith Mountain Lake want a property that can be rented on a short-term basis. There are many homes that will make great rentals, but there are pitfalls that can be easily avoided as well.

First of all, only two of the three counties touching the lake allow short-term rentals. Franklin County made a ruling a number of years ago that forbids short-term rentals of single family homes except in limited situations. There are Franklin County condos and a handful of homes that are grandfathered in and can be rented short-term. It *is*, of course, possible to rent a Franklin County home non-commercially to personal acquaintances on a short-term basis.

Both Bedford and Pittsylvania Counties allow short-term vacation rentals. The right to rent short-term was challenged before the Bedford County Board of Supervisors a few years back, and the Board ruled definitively that rentals are allowed. They did, however, place restrictions on these rentals, and you need to be aware of these rules before calculating the potential cash flow from a home you are considering purchasing.

After the Board ruled in favor of short-term rentals, certain subdivisions in Bedford County tried to disallow rentals based on restrictions against using residential property for a commercial purpose. Several years ago, the State Supreme Court heard this case and ruled in favor of allowing short-term rentals in single family homes provided there were no restrictive covenants prohibiting rentals in that neighborhood.

It is important to know all of the legal and financial issues involved in buying a rental home.

It is also critical to purchase the right home and position it correctly for maximum rental revenue. Next we will consider choosing and staging your rental home.

Section III: SML Investment Properties

How Do I Find the Perfect Rental Home?

If you hope to achieve maximum rental revenue from your investment home here at Smith Mountain Lake, it is critical for you to know what renters are looking for. While the following items do not constitute an exhaustive list, they will provide a start. You may wish to interview a rental agency to confirm what I am saying and get more details. One great home rental agency is RSI Rentals. You can contact Tammy at 866-721-9797. You can also contact Diana at By the Lake Vacation Rentals at (540) 761-8667.

Home Style
Many vacation renters are looking for a home that has a quaint, cottage feel. As a client told me recently, "I am not looking for a house at the lake – I am looking for a lake house." This often includes log homes, cedar homes and the like. Having a lot of windows and a deck facing the water are also important. This does not mean that a house of a different style would not be rentable, but the style of the home gives the first impression to potential renters looking online or through a catalogue.

Slope of the Lot
This can be tricky. It is often expected that a lake house will have a slope, and a slope can contribute to a better view. Some renters want to play volleyball or throw a baseball while on vacation, so they are looking for a gently sloped or flat lot. Renters with elderly family members may want the same. A flat or gently sloped property can certainly contribute to the value of the home as a rental.

Many renters are fine with a steeper slope, but if you buy a home like this to rent, it is important that you fully disclose this in the rental advertising. If a renter pulls up to a home and is surprised by the slope, he may call the agency and switch homes. This would be the worst possible situation for you financially, because your home could be booked (and therefore unavailable to you or others) for many weeks during the summer in which there is actually no revenue generated – and it creates a bad taste in the mouths of all. This will not contribute to a stream of annual return renters, which is the ideal scenario for an investment homeowner.

View

The view from your rental property may be among the most important factors in finding or building the perfect rental home. Home buyers and vacationers often comment about the amazing views we enjoy here at Smith Mountain Lake. Many of the views here are among the best mountain and lake views in the United States. Most rental homes will not provide a picture-perfect view of everything – the lake, the mountains *and* the sunset – but it is important to consider these factors when buying your investment home. Does the home have a long and wide view of open water? A mountain view? Do you have a great view from the home or do you have to go to the dock? Can you trim or remove trees that will enhance the view? These are all important questions to ask when considering buying a rental home. Often a long or wide water view trades off with the next factor.

Cove vs. Main Channel

For renters who think about it, many *assume* they would choose a main channel rental home over one in a cove. (Perhaps they picture a house stuck in the very back of a cove with no view and shallow water, issues that certainly negatively affect the value of a rental.) It is often the case, however, that a home off the main channel will provide as much or more enjoyment for renters and homeowners. Though they sometimes do not enjoy as long or wide of a view, cove homes provide a more peaceful environment and a better location for swimming near the shore. It is important to consider this factor in your choice of a home.

Section III: SML Investment Properties

Water Depth
Water depth is also a bit tricky. While it's important to have good water depth for renters to boat and swim, renters often want a place where children can wade out into the water to swim. The perfect situation is a deep area at the end of the dock and a beach-like area nearby, but since it is rare to have both on the same lot, go for the deep water for the boat as a first priority. If you can get a beach-like area as well, that is a bonus.

Dock
Vacation renters usually want to rent or bring a boat or personal watercraft to the lake. It is therefore important for you to provide a vacant dock slip (or two) for these renters. If you have a boat there, it may be worthwhile to move it to another location if you plan to aggressively rent your home. You may be able to find a service that will pick up and store your boat, making it available for you when needed.

Rental Agency
If you choose to rent your home through one of the many local agencies here at the lake it is important to get a few great referrals and interview more than one agency. Ask them how they prioritize new rental leads. Do they have a stable of other rental homes they fill first? Do they have far more homes than they can fill? How much advertising do they do and where? Do they have a professional staff to service you and the renters? How much do they charge?

You may also choose to use a national rental website, put together your own website, or receive affiliate referrals from other websites that may have renter traffic. A combination of all of these strategies may give you the best opportunity to fill your rental for the maximum number of weeks. If you go with a national rental website, you may need to pay only a nominal annual fee (such as $150) but will need to manage the keys, arrange for cleanings, collect and reimburse security deposits, and handle maintenance items. Even though this can be done remotely, most vacation rental owners choose to go through one of the many local agencies.

Boat
Some vacation homeowners choose to rent out a boat with their rental home. Most agencies choose not to get involved with this due to the liability and hassle. If you are renting your home independently, and if you feel you have appropriate insurance coverage and the ability to deal with the hassle, you may be able to get a return of about $500 per week on a $5,000+ or so investment -- not a bad return. I recommend that you go with a pontoon boat if you decide to do this. I also recommend that you purchase a hefty personal umbrella insurance policy. You can usually get a million dollar policy for a few hundred dollars annually.

Canoe
It may be nice to offer your renters the use of a canoe while staying at your lake home. While the risk is lower than offering a motorized boat, it would certainly be prudent to be sure you have the appropriate insurance coverage for this as well.

Other Amenities
There are a number of other amenities that will help you rent your vacation home for top dollar, higher occupancy, and more return renters. These include a hot tub, foosball table, pool table, ping-pong table, Frisbees, and games. It is also important for you to offer high-speed Internet and cable TV or satellite service. Offering Hulu Plus and Netflix might be an added bonus to attract renters, yet only cost you $20 per month. Think about what you and your family like to do when you rent a vacation home and this will help you in outfitting your home.

Rental Homes Next Door
If you can locate or build rental homes next to one another, you may be able to score big with renters. Many vacationers bring

Section III: SML Investment Properties

several families to the lake. Since Smith Mountain Lake does not have huge eight-bedroom homes for rent like some beach areas, renters often need to rent more than one home. Unfortunately, they may have to coordinate through more than one rental agency or find homes several miles apart, and this deters their vacation enjoyment. If you can solve this problem, it should increase your occupancy, your rates and your profits. Call us for some creative ideas on how to make this happen.

Bedrooms and Septic System
I mentioned that Bedford County had placed restrictions on short-term rentals. These restrictions are based on the number of bedrooms in a rental home, and specifically the number of bedrooms for which the septic system is sized. The rules state that renters can have only two people per bedroom as defined by the septic. Since many homes on the lake have three bedroom septics, most homes are limited to six renters.

This situation can provide an opportunity for you. If you locate a home with lots of extra space (for example with an unfinished basement or area above a garage), you may be able to test the soil and expand the septic system to rent to a larger number of folks. Though this would have a cost, the return should be strong. Having a five- or six-bedroom septic capacity, for example, could set you apart from other rental homes on the lake and dramatically increase your rental rates, occupancy, and return rate.

There are at least four ways to expand a current septic system. Additionally, the sewer system has lines coming through many areas of Bedford County. This could provide another great opportunity for those who purchase these homes compared to those with just septic.

Ask your real estate professional for more information on all of these rental issues. You should also contact various rental agents who can assist you in the most important criteria to look for in your search for an investment home that is perfect for you.

Is There Cash Flow Potential From a Waterfront Rental Home?

One reason that investors have flocked to Smith Mountain Lake is the cash flow potential of a vacation rental. Smith Mountain Lake has become a hot spot for vacationers from all over. Our unique combination of a stunningly beautiful lake, the Blue Ridge Mountains, low taxes, low crime, and proximity to major cities are attracting not only retirees and second homeowners, but also those who choose to spend their weekends and vacations jet skiing, fishing, sailing, hiking and enjoying the peace and solitude here.

Vacation cottages and homes rent from about $750 to $5,000+ weekly. There are at least nine agencies around the lake that manage these homes efficiently. Unfortunately, as discussed above, the largest county here no longer allows short-term rentals, and the other major county has curtailed rentability through septic size restrictions.

The silver lining on this cloud is that supply and demand is on the side of the best remaining and future rental homes. The new restrictions have helped create a situation in which a correctly positioned home can be rented for more than most others. A perfectly designed and positioned rental home can be rented for more than $5,000 a week in prime months and for more weeks than other rental homes on the lake.

While the cash flow potential of a lakefront home provides a great advantage over some investments, it is generally the case that cash flow alone is not a sufficient reason to purchase an investment home here. To my knowledge this is true in most resort areas. It is the great combination of cash flow, equity growth, tax breaks and personal enjoyment that make Smith Mountain Lake a wonderful place to invest.

Section IV:
The Ideal Waterfront Lot

What's in This Section?

Finding the Perfect Waterfront Lot. How Are Lots Valued?

Should I be Concerned About a Septic System?

Can I Split my Waterfront Property into Multiple Parcels?

Finding the Perfect Waterfront Lot. How Are Lots Valued?

Many buyers at Smith Mountain Lake want it all. They want the ideal home on the right lot with a great view in the perfect location, and are willing to pay for it. If this describes you, you may wish to build your own home. If you do plan to build, one of the first and most critical steps is to find the right lot. Keep in mind that a significant portion of the value of a property is based on the inherent value of the lot rather than the quality of the home on it, so your search for a lot should not be taken lightly.

The first step I recommend is to go back and review an earlier section on how property value is derived at Smith Mountain Lake. There I lay out seven key factors that drive the value of *most* waterfront property here. These factors are:

(1) View
(2) Slope
(3) Waterfront (may include shoreline length, water depth, water quality, beach, erosion control, dock, etc.)
(4) Home
(5) Location
(6) Cove versus Main Channel
(7) Size of Lot

Of course your criteria may be different or have a different order, but these seem to be what most buyers value in a waterfront home. Even if your standards are different, please consider the criteria above so your home value will not suffer from value impediments when you want to re-sell it.

Once you have determined your priorities, you will probably begin to research online which waterfront lots are available. Though this is a great way to start your search, you will soon realize it is difficult to get an accurate idea of the quality of a lot solely from the online photos and descriptions. You will need

Section IV: The Ideal Waterfront Lot

plats, numerous photos, information on septic tests, dock permits and more, but much of this information is not available without some digging. One popular online site is Zillow.com, which regularly updates all the listings for MLS properties in the United States. My realty team has put together **SmithMountainHomes.com,** which has details on waterfront lots. Through this site you can look at quite a few premier lots that we and other realty agents have listed here at the lake. Many of these lots include plats and other detailed descriptions and photos. This site is a portal to all the lots and other properties listed on the local MLS. This service (which is provided through the local MLS) allows you to search a property database similar to that used by REALTORS®.

The next step will be for you to engage the services of a REALTOR® who specializes in waterfront lots. There are many Smith Mountain Lake agents who do a fantastic job with waterfront lots. I bought a number of lots through other agents in years past, and I had many good experiences -- and only a few bad. Make sure you ask a lot of questions about their knowledge and skill. I have written a detailed section about how to find a buyer's agent at Smith Mountain Lake, and it will be helpful to review that information as you do your research. I hope you will include the agents from my team in your interview process. You can reach us at 1-877-SML-LOTS (877-765-5687).

When you begin looking at lots, you will find it helpful if the lots are at least partially cleared, well marked at the road and shoreline, and include a plat that is easy to follow. Unfortunately, many lots are not this way. Though this can be frustrating in your search process, it can also provide an opportunity. If you can see past the underbrush and overgrown trees, if you can make your way through the briers, if you can examine survey plats, match GIS maps and aerial photos (available from the county website) to the road and shoreline contours, and imagine the view when the lot is cleared, then you may find a diamond in the rough. Many lots are not "staged" and marketed to easily display their beauty, and buyers are moving too fast to take the time to notice. It is easy to get frustrated and keep moving and miss the lot of your dreams. The opportunity here is compounded in your favor because *you* can be the buyer who finds the lot that other buyers overlooked, the one that sat on the market and dropped in price because the owner did not mark the boundaries, clear a path, or open up the view. I have helped a number of buyers find lots like this. They are out there and it is your job and the job of your Smith Mountain Lake REALTOR® to find them.

Tips for Your Waterfront Lot Search
Here are a few helpful things you can do to facilitate your quest for the perfect waterfront building lot.

- **Apparel**. Many buyers preview lots while dressed in vacation garb. Though you may get hot without your sandals and shorts, it is usually worth it to dress in jeans and boots. This will help you persevere through the underbrush on an overgrown lot and may afford the opportunity to make it to the shoreline when others gave up near the road.
- **Boat and Car**. I strongly recommend that you look at lots by both boat and car. I have found that I can cover about twice as many lots by water. My clients and I can see the approximate view and water depth from a boat without needing to walk the lot. Many lots can be eliminated without spending 20 minutes fighting through the brush. It is also faster to get from lot to lot by boat in most cases. I am able to show lots on the north and south side of the lake within minutes, yet it may take more than an hour round trip just to drive to these lots. I have found that it is best to narrow down lots by boat on the first day of a property search. On the second day, my clients and I have a shorter list of lots to see by car, and I can often get plats and other information to help us walk the top choices the next day.

Section IV: The Ideal Waterfront Lot

- **Measuring Devices.** It is helpful to have measuring devices when reviewing building lots. Because waterfront lots are often irregularly shaped and not well marked, it can be tough to find the boundaries. A laser range finder is helpful in locating the shoreline and roadside boundaries. This wonderful tool is used by golfers and hunters and can be purchased in sporting goods stores. I also recommend that you bring along an outdoor tape measure. These tapes extend a hundred feet or more, and are typically on a spool. They are helpful in measuring off a potential house site. You may be able to borrow one of these from someone in the construction business, or buy one from a construction supply store. Your realty agent may have these items as well.

- **Home plans.** Though it is not necessary to have detailed home plans while searching for a lot, it can be helpful to know the approximate style and size of the home you plan to construct. This will help you measure and envision the home site and the views from the main rooms and decks. Be sure to keep in mind the regulations on setbacks from the sidelines and the lake when making your plans.

- **Depth-Finding Device.** Whether you are looking by land or water, it is important to have a way to gauge the depth of the water off the shoreline at the lot that interests you. Since docks can usually be built well off the shore, you should take depth measurements at about 10-foot intervals from the land where you think you may build a dock. Record these measurements on the plat or information sheet on which you are taking notes. Many boats have depth finders, but you can also use a cheap metal tape measure (you will likely ruin it through rust) or even a tree limb, stick, or rock tied to a string if you're in a pinch. I have done all of the above!

- **Machete.** You will not need this on the vast majority of lots, but may require one to hack your way through the underbrush on an occasional overgrown lot with no path. Of

course you should not cut down trees or nice plants (keep that machete away from your pre-teen boy!), but most lot owners would not mind you hacking away at a few brier bushes along the way.
- **Bug Spray, Drinking Water and Sunscreen.** Although in God's kind providence mosquitoes are mysteriously scarce here at Smith Mountain Lake, we still experience ticks in heavy underbrush. I recommend that clients use bug spray before walking through heavily overgrown lots. You'll need drinking water and sunscreen, although I often seem to forget these items until I am far from a store. Fortunately, there are many waterfront shops at the lake (usually at marinas) and we are typically not far from a store by car.
- **Extension Ladder.** Though I admit I have never done this, I have heard of lot buyers who took an extension ladder to a site to help them envision the view from the level of a proposed main floor of a home. Since most lots are sloped, it can be hard to envision what the view would be from a deck or great room. There can be a 15-foot rise from the ground to the eye level at the building site, and this could reveal either a blocked view due to a neighbor's trees or dock, or an improved longer view of the water or mountains. Without a large, well-placed tree to lean against, however, the extension ladder idea may not work. Has anyone come up with a portable version of those rolling ladders they use at Lowe's?

In summary, I cannot overstate the importance of taking the time to find the lot that is perfect for you. Extensive research, ongoing review online, correspondence with your REALTOR®, and a time commitment to seeing a wide variety of lots by water and on the ground should help ensure that you make the right choice.

Section IV: The Ideal Waterfront Lot

Should I be Concerned About a Septic System?

So you've found the perfect waterfront (or off-water) lot. Your friend, agent or someone else tells you, "You don't need to be concerned about having a new septic percolation test because the lot could never have been divided or sold in the first place without a successful soil percolation test." True or false? Well...both.

Prior to 1982, land could be subdivided and sold as lots without reference to the soil conditions. So now there are some lots throughout Virginia that are unbuildable due to the soil conditions. This is certainly not as uncommon as you may think. As part of an investment group, I have personally tried to buy two waterfront lots that didn't perk (test positive for a septic system) in the past. We had both lots under contract, and on one we had actually only done the soil test as an afterthought to the contract (this was early in my career). If we had not spent the money for the test, we would have owned a beautiful waterfront point lot that would have been useful for planting flowers and camping and docking our boat, but little more. And we would have been $200,000 poorer, with no easy way out.

In 1982, the rules changed. Developers had to prove that every lot would allow a septic system or be within access to public sewer. So you might assume any lot developed since then will be suitable for a septic system, correct? Well, again, yes...and no. In 2001, the rules for septic field sizes changed, making it tougher to get a system on lots with marginal soil. (Septic trench bottoms had been allowed 12 inches above bedrock, but this limit was increased to a minimum of 18 inches, which became a big deal for some lots throughout Virginia.) So there are some lots that were developed after 1982 that were fine until 2001 and are not acceptable today. A lot owner can show you a successful perk test from the 90s, but this does not mean you can get a system on the lot today.

This became an issue recently when a client of mine went to purchase a waterfront lot. The owner had an old permit showing that the lot could support a three-bedroom septic system. The client followed my advice and got a new test. Then another test. And a review. This lot would not allow any septic system at all. Another near financial disaster averted.

Fortunately, with additional hurdles come additional innovations. There are a number of alternative septic designs that will allow most of these difficult lots to have the benefit of a septic system. I have contacts with engineers and consultants who design and install these systems and we sell lots every year that require them.

Another alternative is to buy nearby lots for the installation of a system. One of my clients got a great deal on a non-perking waterfront lot and bought two large inexpensive off-water lots across the street with excellent soil. Now he has three lots with three home building sites and three septic sites. He stands to make a few hundred thousand dollars if he sells these lots or builds spec homes for resale.

An additional alternative is to approach a neighbor to buy rights to a corner of a nearby property to install a system there. A last possibility is to tap into the county sewer system.

By the way, this septic system issue can provide a great opportunity for smart investors to purchase lots at below-market value. Call us if you would like to discuss this further.

Section IV: The Ideal Waterfront Lot

Can I Split my Waterfront Property Into Multiple Parcels?

Most buyers here are also astute investors. Perhaps you are one of them. Investors often want me to help them find a property that can be divided, or a property that will allow the construction of an additional cottage or home. Is this possible?

This is not possible for most properties. There are little known or understood rules, however, that allow many properties to be split into multiple parcels. For example, when my mother moved here from Ohio, I was able to split off an acre for her to live on as part of a property that would otherwise *not* have been sub-dividable. This rule is called the Family Exemption, and although it is a great option for the right situation, it can also be a mine field if not handled properly.

There is another potentially remarkable opportunity to subdivide property that may be available. This prospect was made possible by installation of a sewage system on the Bedford County side of the lake. It is likely that a similar system will eventually open up these opportunities in Franklin County as well. In summary, the rules for subdividing property may be less restrictive in some cases due to the availability of public water and sewer. From a practical perspective, it is often possible to increase the density of buildings in an area that does not need private septics and wells. This can also help beautify a building site because trees will not have to be removed for these other services. Note that the availability of public sewer is still limited to a small percentage of the waterfront lots here, which is probably good for the lake as a whole. Contact a realty agent to learn more about how this could benefit you.

Note that if a lot with *less than* 200 feet of waterfrontage is split, each resulting lot (with under 100 feet of shoreline) will not have the right to an individual dock. The Shoreline Management Plan allows for a shared two-slip dock in these cases, provided that the *total* shoreline from the two lots is at least 150 linear feet. This is not ideal, but may be worth it in some cases.

Section V:

Building a New Home

What's in This Section?

I Want to Build a Home. Is There an Ideal Mountain-Lake Home Style?

How Close to the Water Can I Build My New Home?

Is it Tough to Obtain a Building Permit at SML?

Building a Home: What Will It Cost? How Long Will It Take?

Building a Home: What About Modular Homes?

Building a Home: Should I Add a Basement or a Garage?

How Do I Design My Basement for Maximum Enjoyment and Resale Value?

Building a Home: How Do I Find a Contractor?

Building a Boathouse or Dock: What Will It Cost? How Do I Find a Contractor?

How Do I Finance My New Home Construction?

Can I Build Multiple Homes on One Property? Can I Build a Guesthouse on My Property?

I Want to Build a Home. Is There an Ideal Mountain-Lake Home Style?

Is there a perfect home design for Smith Mountain Lake? Since I deal in waterfront lots and have built seven homes here, I am often asked for advice on plans that work well for waterfront homes. I used to send clients to Lowe's or online to look at home plans that are used everywhere else. These plans often had to be modified to take advantage of the spectacular waterfront and mountain views that Smith Mountain Lake offers. Frank Betz and Southern Living were two of my favorite sources for plans, and I even helped design two homes myself.

More recently, however, I have discovered an amazing source for waterfront home designs. Lest you think I exaggerate, I will tell you that seven of the last eight lot buyers I have assisted were blown away by these designs, and several are planning to have these homes built for them. These homes are designed to maximize lake and mountain views, and are completely customizable. It is likely that you will find at least a variation of your dream lake home among the wide variety of homes in their catalogue.

These homes are distributed through a national company called Viceroy Homes. Viceroy sells its plans through independent distributors and builders nationwide. If you would like to learn more about these homes, you may look online at **Viceroy.com** or call me for information on a distributor. Viceroy has a beautiful catalogue to see these mountain-lake homes for yourself. Even if you never build one, the catalogue makes a beautiful coffee table book!

Section V: Building A New Home

How Close to the Water Can I Build My New Home?

As you look around the lake, have you noticed that some homes are built right at the edge of the water? Some are even built out over the shoreline. If this is what you want, you will need to find your home through the resale market. This practice is no longer permitted for new construction at Smith Mountain Lake, but existing homes are grandfathered in. You may be happy to learn that these homes come on the market from time to time, yet they are actually not too popular with buyers. I know of at least two that have sat on the market for some time at reasonable prices. I remember a nice 3-bedroom/2 bath home built right next to the water for $499,000. Initially I thought it would sell quickly but it sat on the market through a few seasons.

While homes built right at the water's edge are generally not that popular, having a short distance from the home to the lake is often a significant factor in the enjoyment and value of a Smith Mountain Lake home. So how close to the shore can you build a new home? There are three relevant factors.

The first factor is a regulation that is part of Appalachian Power's Shoreline Management Plan. It states that a home must be built above the 800-foot (above sea level) contour line. The area below this level is under the control of the power company.

The second factor is a regulation imposed by the county building departments. It states that a home (including a rear deck above the ground level) must be at least a certain distance back horizontally from the vertical line that extends up from the shoreline at "full pond" (normal full lake level). This horizontal distance is 25 feet in Bedford County, 20 feet in Franklin County, and 35 feet in Pittsylvania County. This means that when the lake is at its normal full level of 795 feet above sea level, a vertical line is extended from the edge of the shore. Then a horizontal line is extended from this line to where it meets the ground on the lot. At the point where this horizontal line is at least 25 feet long in Bedford County, or 20 feet long in Franklin County, or 35 feet in Pittsylvania County, this rule is satisfied. Using simple triangle geometry, this point is typically met at about 26 to 30 feet from the water *for most normally sloping lots* in Bedford County (approximately 21 to 25 in Franklin and approximately 36 to 40 in Pittsylvania). This point can be farther from the water on a much steeper lot.

The third rule has to do with the 100-year floodplain. This floodplain is at 803 feet above sea level (some still measure it at 802.7 feet, however most surveyors and others measure it at 803 feet). This is 8 vertical feet above the lake's normal full level. You are allowed to build a home above the 800-foot contour, and at least 20, 25 or 35 horizontal feet from the shoreline (see above), but if your home extends into the 100-year floodplain you will need to purchase flood insurance. This will be an annual expense, so think hard about whether you want to burden yourself and the future buyers of your home this way. Check with an insurance agent to find out what this may cost.

If you want to get close to the water, you will need to plan to build the closest point of your new home in a location that meets these requirements at a minimum. Note that while the rear deck of your home counts in this analysis, any patios (flush to ground level) or stairs extending from the home or deck do not. You are not "penalized" for these structures.

Is there a certain type of lot that causes problems in meeting these requirements? Yes! While many buyers want a virtually flat lot, this can result in problems meeting the shore setback discussed above. A flatter lot will result in the closest location (usually by a small amount) to the water using the geometry of the 20-, 25- or 35-foot horizontal rule discussed above. However, a flatter lot may result in a 100-year flood plain level that encroaches far into the lot. Recall that a home must be built at least 8 vertical feet above the lake's full level to avoid flood insurance. In rare cases on a virtually flat lot, this could be a

Section V: Building A New Home

long distance from the shore and may even be near the front of the lot.

The danger in this situation is that a very flat lot may result in a building site that is in the 100-year flood plain. I know of a lady who bought her virtually flat point lot years ago for an amazing price. She decided not to build on it, but has held onto it as an investment. Now she needs to sell it. The new survey stakes told the sad tale. The stakes for the 800-foot contour pushed the home site far from the shoreline, and the stakes for the 100-year flood plain are near the road. Most of the lot is in the AEP Project Boundary or the floodplain. There may barely be room to construct a home on the lot, and the home will certainly need to be built in the 100-year floodplain. She will need professional assistance to see how to place a home on her lot.

Fortunately, this is a lake constructed within Blue Ridge Mountain ridges and peaks. As a result, the vast majority of waterfront lots have some slope and are not subject to the dangers discussed above. You need to be aware of these rules before you purchase a waterfront lot at Smith Mountain Lake. If you have any doubts, it is certainly worth the expense of getting a survey on the waterfront lot of your dreams.

By the way, there *may* be ways to mitigate the issues that arise with a flat lot. Some lot owners have carted in truckloads of fill dirt to build up the lot from the road part way down to the shore. This allowed for a building site and a walkout basement on an otherwise nearly flat lot. Though it may be a good idea to use fill dirt to build up a lot and to build a basement, you will generally *not* be allowed to bring in fill dirt to extend the building area into the current, natural 100-year floodplain. Though some lot owners have reportedly done this without permission, you should check with the county planning and zoning/building inspection department to evaluate the situation for your lot.

One last note... If you want to avoid the floodplain and flood insurance, you must not only build your home above the stakes for the 803' contour, but you must also be certain that your basement floor is above this level vertically. It would be possible for you to build a home above the floodplain stakes, but to excavate your basement into the ground below, and thus back *into*, the floodplain. Be sure that your surveyor, excavator, and builder are aware of any concerns you have in this area.

Section V: Building A New Home

Is It Tough to Obtain a Building Permit at SML?

Many property owners at Smith Mountain Lake come from urban areas with regulations that make it difficult to construct or alter a building on their property. These folks are happily surprised when they learn how easy it is to obtain building permits in the three counties touching Smith Mountain Lake. Franklin County, Bedford County, and Pittsylvania County are rural areas that have not yet been raided by big city bureaucrats whose goal is to make life miserable for people with the resources to build on their private property.

Typically, the application process for a building permit, including a septic permit, takes a day or so. You will need drawings of the building you plan to construct and a picture of where it will be erected on your lot. Usually, you can begin building immediately after the permit is issued. As necessary, building inspectors are called in to assure that your building is built in compliance with international building codes. This is important for your safety and enjoyment, as well as for the benefit of whoever may purchase your home in the future.

A realty agent and/or builder should be able to assist you in applying for building permits in addition to well and septic permits.

Building a Home: What Will It Cost? How Long Will It Take?

Since my realty team has a significant focus on waterfront lots, we are often asked about the cost of building a home here. There are many builders in the area, and the prices range widely. This is probably similar to where you live.

I have owned a small construction company, interviewed many builders, and worked with many lot owners who have had homes built here, and I can give you some ideas. But it is just an estimate since there are many variables. The variables in building costs may include:

- The style and size of the home
- The type of construction
- The options and upgrades
- The contractor
- Whether you build on a cost-plus or contract basis
- Work performed by you, the owner (if any)
- The type of septic system and water supply
- The steepness of the lot at the building site, driveway, and access point to the lake
- Whether or not you finish the basement
- Costs of building materials at the time of construction
- Timing and financing for construction
- Many more variables particular to your situation

I have heard quotes and actual building costs ranging from $110 to $200 per square foot on the main (above ground level) floors. I know of eco-friendly homes that cost *much* more than this. Most homes come in between $125 and $175 per square foot for the main floors.

The basement can usually be finished for about $25 to $50 per square foot. This can be more expensive in the event of

Section V: Building A New Home

significant upgrades and somewhat less if you buy the materials and do the work yourself. So it is possible that you could build a 1,500 square-foot ranch for $195,000 (about $130 per square foot). Then, for an additional $60,000 or so, you could double the square footage by finishing a walkout basement. So you would have a 3,000 square-foot home for $255,000, an average cost of $85 per square foot. One great benefit of this strategy is that the REALTORS® and buyers in this market (unlike some markets) generally consider finished square footage in a walkout basement as part of the total square footage of the home.

Timing
Although it is possible to do it more quickly, it generally takes longer than you expect to build a home. Similar to where you live, things just take longer than planned.

I recommend that you plan for it to take about a year to build a new home. It can be done in much less time, but you need to factor in time to select and modify drawings, arrange financing, deal with weather problems, and much more. If you select a great builder, that builder may be backed up a number of months or a year. One of my favorite builders at the lake is backed up 13 months to start a new home. Is he worth it? Absolutely – if you can wait 18 months to move into your home.

It should take a builder approximately five to seven months to finish your home once he gets started. I know of homes that have been finished in as little as three months, but I also know of a large home in Waverly that took a few years to build. The next section tells of a way to save time on the construction of your new home.

Building a Home: What About Modular Homes?

Some newcomers to Smith Mountain Lake are surprised at the large number and variety of modular homes at the lake and around the area. Should you consider building a modular home? Are these just fancy trailers? What are the pros and cons of a modular home? What is the resale value of a modular versus a stick-built home?

It is true that modular homes used to be similar to doublewide trailers. Like trailers, they were built on steel frames and constructed on crawl spaces. Like trailers, they were mass manufactured with stock floor plans and inexpensive materials. Like doublewides, they were delivered in two sections and joined together on-site. Some of the older model modulars seem to differ from doublewides only in the pitch of the roof – 7/12 versus 5/12 pitch.

But modular homes have come a long way since those days. In fact, quality modular homes have far more in common with stick-built homes than with trailers. Like regular stick-built homes, quality modular homes are now built on regular foundations (typically a basement in this area), not on steel frames. Like stick-built homes, modular homes now offer a variety of floor plans and building materials. Also like stick-built homes, modular homes offer Cape Cod styles and two-story models. Modular homes offer roof pitches between 7/12 (standard) and 12/12 (story and a half or Cape Cod style).

Modular homes are now constructed according to the same standards and building codes as regular stick-built homes and are built to travel down the road at 60 miles per hour! Often it is hard to determine if an existing home is modular or stick-built. One way to tell is by the thickness of the joining wall, the center wall between the sections. There is really nothing cheap about a quality modular home. The only things that could be cheap are the same things that are often cheap in any new home (the plumbing fixtures and cabinets, for example). By the same token, these same items can be upgraded in a modular home,

Section V: Building A New Home

just like in a regular home. One local modular builder now offers standard nine-foot ceilings, solid-surface countertops and much more.

Some of the advantages of quality modular homes are:

- **Speed of construction.** Modular homes should be ready to move into more quickly than a typical stick-built home. This is partially dependent on the backlog in the factory as well as the ability of the on-site contractor (or you) to finish the job in a timely manner.
- **Precision of construction.** Modular homebuilders should have an advantage in the area of precision and consistency. A board cut on a factory band saw will more likely be cut straighter and more precisely than one cut on a sawhorse on a muddy hillside. A hundred boards will be cut more consistently on a factory floor than on a typical job site.
- **Weather.** Everyone knows the variety of problems weather can cause for a construction project. Contractors can be backed up for weeks or months due to bad weather in the off-season. This can cause inconsistency of employees as workers come and go due to weather and other issues common to the construction industry. Furthermore, the potential damage to the home due to weather is hard to gauge. I was on the site of a home during framing and wondered what the long-term impact of the 2-inch layer of ice and snow on the particleboard floor would be. This is not an issue in the construction of a modular home. Except for a few hours after the home is delivered, the interior should not be exposed to the elements. This can only be an advantage.
- **Quality control.** Workers on some construction crews may come and go, viewing their roles as a day laborer. Some of them, as in other professions, struggle with drug and alcohol abuse. But employees at a modular home plant usually view their positions as permanent jobs. While they may also struggle with substance abuse and absenteeism, a modular

manufacturer typically has several layers of quality control that have a better chance of catching mistakes.

- **Cost.** It is widely believed that there are cost savings in building a modular home. This can be true, but like everything else the cost can vary widely. All things being equal, there may be cost savings associated with modular construction. One advantage is derived from the fact that the cost of a modular home can be estimated more accurately than a site-built home in some cases. Even a modular home, however, has a significant on-site component, so the total cost may not be less expensive than that of stick building.

To my knowledge, the only disadvantage of a modular home is that there may be limitations in layout and design. While modular builders can use a wide variety of plans, there are just some designs they cannot accomplish, and an onsite builder is required. Even the most customized modular company in the area has a stick-built division for those times when modular just won't work.

It may seem by my comments that I would only recommend a modular home. That is not the case. There may be great craftsmanship or serious problems with either construction mode, but there are typically fewer risks with a factory-built home than an *average* site-built home.

There are four major modular home factories and several more distributors within an hour of the lake. I had six modular homes constructed for resale between 1992 and 1995. My family is considering building a new home in the near future and we are already planning to interview both stick-builders and modular builders. I have talked to a few of each already and can see it may be a hard decision. When it is time for you to choose, please check references, and be sure to get advice from trustworthy local sources. Local modular home factories include: Southern Heritage, Clayton Homes, Freedom Homes, and Mod-U-Kraf.

Section V: Building A New Home

Building a Home: Should I Add a Basement or Garage?

Many lot owners preparing to build at Smith Mountain Lake ask these questions. Some folks come here from areas such as Raleigh, where garages are a must and basements are virtually unheard of, so they assume it is the same here. It is critical for these individuals to consult with locals in the know to compare the market realities here to where they live.

Recently, there were two beautiful neighboring new homes on the market in Franklin County. For the size and price range, these homes were exquisite in their detail and style. I would be happy to live in either of them. They were priced well and their prices had dropped a few times in the year or so they sat on the market. What was wrong?

Both homes had a nice two-car garage but both were built on slabs. This is generally a big no-no in this area. It is not that slabs or crawl spaces are bad, but most new or resale homes on a full unfinished basement cost just a little bit more than the same homes on a slab. The vast majority of homes here, even some doublewides, are on basements. So given the choice, virtually no one would choose not to have a basement.

Even if you don't want a basement, please consider building one and leaving it unfinished so you don't harm the future resale on your home. I just sold a lot for more than $800,000 to a family who just didn't want or need a basement. I think I convinced them that for the minimal increased cost, it would dramatically help them to have a basement rather than a crawl space if they decide to sell the home. This is especially true in that price range (the lot plus home will be in the $1.5 million range).

With regard to the basement, the rolling terrain here often makes it ideal to build a walkout basement. Perhaps this is called a daylight basement where you live. This is a basement that opens straight out into the yard. It allows for views through sliding glass doors and windows. If done well, a basement like this can look much like the regular level of the home, not like the dungeons you may picture from days gone by.

Even if you don't finish your basement, please consider putting in large egress windows in the sides and large sliding glass doors on the back. This will allow the next owners to picture the possibility of finishing the basement to their tastes.

My friend and I recently bought a home to rehab and flip. The basement had small, high windows, but it could have easily had egress windows (probably minimal cost when constructed). If we decide to finish a room there, we have the added cost and hassle of tearing up the wall and installing a larger window. This would have been so much better, and more valuable if done upfront.

You should also consider plumbing the basement for a bathroom in the event that you or the next owner wishes to finish it. By the way, if you have an unfinished basement and are trying to sell your home, it may be a good idea to go in with chalk and mark off outlines of where bedrooms, bathroom or family room could be placed. This will help potential buyers envision the possibilities. Get a local REALTOR®, interior designer or builder to assist you in this process.

Section V: Building A New Home

How Do I Design My Basement for Maximum Enjoyment and Resale Value?

Whether you are finishing the basement now or not, it is critical that you design it for the best possible layout. If possible, this means that the stairs should go down one of the end walls and that the bathroom should not be plumbed along the back wall. Usually a great spot for a bathroom is toward the front wall of the basement, either in a corner or the middle. I also recommend placing the heating, air conditioning, well tank, and hot water heater out of the way -- preferably together near the front wall in a corner. If you finish the basement, you will want this to be out of the way of the main room or the bedrooms.

I also recommend that you spend the extra money to get high ceilings in a basement. When the basement is finished, you want to be sure that the ceiling is at least eight feet high, taking into account the drywall, ductwork and beams.

There was a nice home for sale in a prestigious subdivision. Homes all around it were selling for approximately $1 million, but the owners couldn't sell it for a long time even though it was priced in the $700,000 range. My buyer clients couldn't understand it when they saw it online. They quickly understood however, when they went to the basement. The ceilings were only seven feet high in most places, and I think they may have been even less in some spots. Though it was finished nicely, it felt closed in, and even prospective buyers who liked the home were scared away by the potential problems with resale. (Part of the job of a good buyer's agent is to point out problems with future resale, and apparently most agents did their job because the home didn't sell for a long time.)

There was another home for sale in a nearby subdivision about the same time. This home had basement ceilings as high as 12 feet. It was so open that it felt like a great room. The home sold quickly.

If you have the opportunity, try to design your basement without supporting columns. Though this may cost a bit more, it will be well worth it to not have to work around columns in laying out the basement. This can be accomplished by supporting the upstairs with trusses that span the width of the basement.

When we finished my basement, we were plagued with all of the problems I pointed out above. First, the stairs come right down the middle of the home. This limits the layout of the basement and virtually precludes us from having a large, open living area there. Second, the main floor is only about 8 feet above the basement floor, so after dropping in ductwork and drywall, the height of the basement ceiling in a few spots is less than ideal. Third, the house is supported by columns that dramatically limit our furniture placement throughout the lower level. Fourth, the HVAC and other equipment are right in the middle of the basement rather than off in a corner. The folks who built this home did many things right, but the basement design wasn't among them. We feel very thankful to have a basement, however, unlike our friends in Raleigh and Virginia Beach.

Section V: Building A New Home

Building a Home: How Do I Find a Contractor?

If you are building a home in this area, finding the right contractor is a critical issue -- especially if you are from outside the area. My family moved here from the Detroit area in 1998 and we needed a builder. We were frankly surprised that some of the builders here didn't seem to have cell phones, brochures, or business cards at the time. It seemed a bit odd, to say the least. Fortunately, things have changed a lot, and this is no longer the case for the most part. However, some builders still manage their operation like a dropout from life looking for something to do, while other builders operate professionally. Choose the latter. (Go ahead... call me Captain Obvious.)

I once had a builder tell me that, "all buyers are liars." He was referring to the allegation that all clients speak badly of builders after the construction is complete. He said there were so many factors that go wrong in the building of a new home that this was inevitable. Another builder told me that all of his clients are angry with him for the last part of the building process, when the final details and costs are being ironed out. I don't believe it must be this way, and have assisted many clients who have great experiences and become friends with their builders. Even so, many homeowners are unhappy with their builder, and describe the construction process as a nightmare. I don't want this to happen to you, and it doesn't need to.

It is common to get sweet-talked into using the first builder you speak with (just like those dog-gone REALTORS®). This is easy to do since some of the initial conversations with builders take a lot of your valuable time, especially if you don't live in the area. This *might* work out okay, but take a few more simple steps first.

First, talk in detail to your REALTOR® and others from the area. Ask them to provide the names of their top builders and ask why they recommend them. Make sure they are not just recommending a friend, neighbor, or a few names from the phonebook. If you are buying a lot in a newer neighborhood, you may be able to speak with neighbors who have recently had a home built. (You will be amazed at how friendly the folks are here in Southwest Virginia. You can just walk up to their door or catch them taking a walk.) Ask them who they dealt with and take good notes if you hear a name that is spoken of positively. If you find a few neighbors who loved one builder, and recommend him, you'll have a good candidate to interview.

Second, interview the builder face-to-face. You will learn a lot about a builder this way. How does he manage his personal life? Was he on time for the meeting? What is the condition of his vehicle? Ask him for a list of homes he has built and take a drive by. Ask him what his relationship with past clients is like, and then ask for a list of references. Call the references and ask detailed questions such as the cost and timing of the finished project compared with what was estimated or promised. Ask the builder where most of his supplies are purchased. Go into that store and ask the staff or manager whether the bills are paid on time and if the builder's business seems to be run in a professional manner. Even if the employee feels compelled to speak positively about their customer (the builder), you can often read a lot in their responses. Ask the builder for addresses where building is in process. Check out the job site after hours or on a weekend. Does it look sloppy and carelessly managed or neat and tidy?

Third, if all of the above check out, talk to the top two builders about their approach to pricing and cost. I recommend narrowing the builder down to your top choice or two before asking for a detailed bid. This will be more fair to the contractor and provide you with a more accurate estimate. It would be good at this point to know which cost approach the builder prefers and why. There are two main approaches: contract-bid or cost-plus. You need to think through the differences in using each approach.

Section V: Building A New Home

In a contract-bid approach, the builder should provide an extremely detailed breakdown of the finished items included in the bid and the factors that would cause the cost to go up or down. Note the cost of expensive, highly variable items such as cabinets, flooring and lighting. A great builder should be able to anticipate the level of quality and cost of items in his bid based on his experience, conversations with you, and the final value of the home on the lot. If he is honest, he will not have bid these at a low level just to get your business. (This will take some homework on your part to anticipate the price range to expect for these items.) There are builders out there who can provide a bid per square foot, but once *you* have chosen a long list of upgrades midstream the cost ends up 50% higher. They may try to make it sound like it was your fault for choosing "so many upgrades," but the truth is that they are responsible for not bidding the home more honestly upfront. This issue should be discussed with the builder and his references in advance. A contract bid builder must add some cushion for contingencies such as weather problems or increases in the cost of materials. This cushion can turn into extra profit for the builder if things go well, and on the surface, it seems like this approach may result in a higher price to you.

Enter the cost-plus approach! Builders using this methodology argue that you, the customer, should not have to pay for that extra cushion in the event that things don't go wrong. At the same time, they don't want to bear the financial liability in the event that things go awry. So they give you their best guess on how much the home will cost based again on their experience, conversations with you, and the final value of the home on the lot. Then they provide you with detailed invoices along the way showing their costs of labor and materials. Their profit is simply a matter of adding a set percentage to the cost (the "plus" in cost-plus). A typical profit range is 15% to 20%. (The builder may argue that he would figure in 30% if doing a contract-bid in order to account for unexpected problems.) It seems like this open-book approach would be less costly to the client and fair to everyone.

I am not willing to say that there is one correct approach in all circumstances. It is highly dependent on the builder, your level of knowledge and involvement, the weather, the type of lot, and much more. I will say, however, that most of the problems and dissatisfied clients I encounter are in the cost-plus arena. The cost-plus approach puts the risk of all problems on you, the buyer. It would be great if there are no significant problems, but you need to know something right upfront: THERE WILL BE PROBLEMS!

As an inexperienced home buyer, do you want to bear this risk or do you want to allow it to be borne by the person who deals with these types of issues daily, and has for years? Another criticism of the cost-plus approach is that it is like giving your builder your checkbook. Do you really trust him *that* much? What motivation will he have to get several detailed bids for a component of the job? Will he fight to get the lowest price for the electrical work, for example? Will he tell you about a wholesale outlet where you can save 25% on the lighting and plumbing fixtures? Or, due to the cost-plus profit arrangement, might he even be hoping that the costs will come in higher? Do the math. Twenty-percent of a bigger number is…a bigger number! (I got A's in math.) If you go with a cost-plus approach, you better know your builder extremely well. And if he is that close of a friend, you better realize that he *may* not be a friend after the process is complete.

Is it obvious that I generally favor the contract-bid approach? You need to make your own decision on this, but whatever you decide, you can see that you should be willing to spend a *significant amount of due diligence upfront* before choosing a builder. Ask a lot of questions. Call all references. Find other homes the builder has constructed and talk with those owners. Much of this process can be shortened by looking for word-of-mouth references. If you start your search in the phone book or chamber of commerce directory, you will greatly

Section V: Building A New Home

lengthen the process and set yourself up for possible frustration. Bottom line: Seek counsel! Proverbs 15:22 says, "Without counsel plans fail, but with many advisers they succeed."

Fourth, before you get started on your home, talk through with your builder what items are included and not included in the bid or pricing estimate. A simple example is landscaping and sidewalks. I have known of many clients who didn't think about this item, and had a picture of a beautifully manicured new lawn to go with their beautiful new home. But when moving day came, they were faced with trying to figure out how to keep the mud off the new carpets. These folks often spend many thousands of dollars to finish what they assumed was part of the package. I am not suggesting that this is the fault of the builder, but only that these types of things need to be discussed in advance.

I know of many builders here in the lake area that appear to be competent and honest. In case I have discouraged or frightened you away from building, I want to highlight a bit of what I know about two local builders so you will know that there is hope! They are very different, yet both have a long list of extremely happy clients and are proud of the homes they have constructed around the lake area.

The first builder moved here from metro Washington, D.C. He has a background managing a commercial and residential construction company and runs his company like a well-oiled machine. He works out of a nice office and has a professional staff. After he gets an idea of your scope and project, he can tell you the date that he will break ground as well as the scheduled completion date. (He averages about 10 days early on his completion estimates.) He will provide you with a beautiful folder with a detailed list of past clients *including their phone numbers.* Think about that. You can call any one of them and ask them to verify what you are hearing from him. His presentation folder also details promised versus actual completion dates of all the homes he has built in the past decade, as well as the percentage over or under his original bid was from the final total cost of the home. He prides himself on getting to know his clients in advance, and bidding their homes in such a range as to minimize upgrade change orders along the way. The average upgrades for his buyers are a few percent or less. He is not only a builder, but an artist and an architect, and he provides helpful design and money-saving ideas to his clients. Once you choose him, it will take at least a few months to get under way since he spends considerable time in the design and bid process and typically has a backlog of clients. (As a side note, this builder believes that the cost-plus approach is akin to robbery. He works only under fixed-bid arrangements.) He is not the cheapest builder in town, but his clients say his services are worth every penny.

A second builder I wish to highlight seems different in many ways. He was born and raised here in the sticks and has the accent to prove it. He started building around the lake as a young man in the mid-1960's. You may not be impressed with him when you first speak to him on the phone, but you will be impressed when you see any of the homes he has built. The attention to detail and quality are unsurpassed in anything I have seen here at the lake. Many of his standard features would be considered upgrades for other builders. He has a long list of satisfied clients. I talked to one family that hired him to build their last two homes, and they say they hope he will build their third. They would never use anyone else. (This is rare in this business.) Real estate agents are happy to highlight his name in listings in which he was the builder. He has people waiting for him to start their homes, even in slow markets. You would likely not go wrong if you chose him as your builder.

These are just two brief profiles to give you hope that you *can* find a great builder here at Smith Mountain Lake. This should also highlight something else. Out of the many builder ads in the local phone books or Smith Mountain Lake Chamber of Commerce, you would probably *not* have chosen one of these two to interview. You may have ended up spending a lot of time, energy and a year or so of frustration that could have been

Section V: Building A New Home

avoided if you sought professional advice and carefully checked builder references. I didn't come up with these (and several other great) builders' shining profiles overnight. You shouldn't expect to either. You may choose the wrong REALTOR®, the wrong closing attorney, or the wrong mortgage loan officer, but whatever you do, do not choose the wrong builder.

Building a Boathouse or Dock: What Will It Cost?

Homeowners in the 1960's and 1970's sometimes constructed simple piers or floating docks at their waterfront. This reflected the simple trailers or cottages prevalent at that time. Now it is common for homeowners to build more extravagant docks. Some new boathouses cost more than the older homes on the lake!

As a result of the high price of waterfront homes and the concern that future regulations may limit the size of future boathouses, most new dock construction is at or near the limit of current regulations. As a reminder, most lots with under 300 feet of waterfront can have a new dock of up to 1,500 square feet with two covered boat slips and any number of personal watercraft (aka Sea Doo) lifts. Most lots with more than 300 feet of shoreline can have a new dock of up to 2,250 square feet and three covered slips. Lots with more shoreline can have larger docks.

Due to wide variations in design, contractors and building materials, the price of dock construction varies widely. A single slip dock can vary from $20,000 to $35,000 or more. Most double slip docks range between $40,000 and $75,000. Most triple slip docks range between $50,000 and $90,000. Most new docks would include a floater, a storage building and standard lifts that can handle a boat up to about 6,000 pounds. Composite decking and rails may add about $4,000 to $8,000 to the cost of most docks; a party deck (which I highly recommend) may add about $5,000; and personal watercraft lifts about $1,500 to $2,500 each. Adding a party deck with all composite decking should add about $10,000 to $13,000 to the basic cost. Each standard mechanical hoist is approximately $2,000+ installed. If you are one of the few unfortunate people who live in an area of heavy rock near the shoreline, you may need steel pilings. Steel pilings will add about $12,000 or so for a typical two-slip dock.

One of the best ways to design your dock is to take a few hours out by boat and take photos of some of your favorite

Section V: Building A New Home

docks to share with your dock builder. Note that once you choose your dock builder, let them draw up the plans and submit them to AEP for the permit. They are familiar with the regulations and the personnel there, and can usually obtain a permit in two to three weeks. It may take you much longer to do the same.

Choosing a dock builder is much easier than choosing a homebuilder, and the stakes are not quite as high. There are far fewer to choose from and there are several great ones here. There are not as many things that can go wrong. The process of choosing a dock builder is much the same as choosing a homebuilder, but not nearly as lengthy: Ask a REALTOR®, get references, ask a lot of questions, check out their work, and give them small tests to see if they keep their promises. Be cautious.

How Do I Finance My New Home Construction?

Most residential lenders have programs that provide financing for new home construction. These lenders typically work from a draw system and provide payments directly to contractors based on the completion of certain benchmark items. The completion of these items is verified by an appraiser hired by the bank to perform on-site inspections at various intervals.

Typical loans fund about 80% of the cost of construction. At the end of the construction process, you will have a lot loan of up to 80% and a construction loan for about the same. At the time of a certificate of occupancy (the county inspector's acknowledgement that the home is complete), it is standard for owners to roll both of these loans into a permanent financing vehicle such as a 30-year mortgage.

Section V: Building A New Home

Can I Build Multiple Homes on One Property? Can I Build a Guesthouse on My Property?

Many property owners here consider adding a second dwelling such as a cottage, second home, or over-the-garage apartment to their property. A friend of mine just sold a large waterfront home with an additional one bedroom/one bath cottage close to the water. Last year, I sold a home with a large detached garage that had two additional bedrooms, a kitchen, living room and bath -- all over the garage. One of my new clients has come up with a brilliant way to add a guest cottage near the main home on his waterfront lot, which was approved by the county, although this wouldn't work everywhere.

Though the ordinances have been dramatically tightened, there are still ways to put a second home on certain properties or to build a living space over a garage. In fact, one of the great waterfront properties for sale on the lake seems to have the potential for a complete second home and dock to be built on it. The opportunities are situation-specific, so please contact a REALTOR® or the county planning and zoning office to review your particular situation.

Section VI:

Purchasing Property at Smith Mountain Lake

What's in This Section?

I Can't Afford It... Or Can I? Some Creative Ways to Finance a Waterfront Home at Smith Mountain Lake

Seller and Buyer, Sittin' in a Tree...What is a Love Letter? Should I Write One? Why and How?

Do I Need a Home Inspection?

Do I Need a Property Survey?

I Want to Buy a Home at the Lake, but I Dread Paying for Flood Insurance. Will I Need it?

How is the Dock Transferred to the New Owner at Closing?

How Do I Close on my Smith Mountain Lake Property?

I Can't Afford It... Or Can I? Some Creative Ways to Finance a Waterfront Home at Smith Mountain Lake

Many buyers wonder whether they will be able to qualify for a mortgage for a second home here. Some wish they could access investment funds they could use for property at the lake. Because I have worked with clients and done some investing myself over the years, I have learned strategies that can assist buyers in funding a second home.

Please note that I am not a tax adviser or licensed mortgage professional. (I don't even play one on TV.) The information discussed below is intended only to raise issues that you need to pursue with the assistance of licensed professionals.

Tax Deferred Exchange

The Internal Revenue Service has a provision that allows investment properties to be sold and exchanged for a new property without taxation on the gains from the exchanged property. This is called an IRS Section 1031 Exchange, and is also referred to as a like-kind exchange. Though the name implies a swap of properties with another property owner, the exchange is actually between your current investment property (referred to as the "relinquished property") and a new one (the "replacement property"). (While it is rare to find two property owners who wish to do an actual direct swap, I was involved in a swap of waterfront lots like this here last year, and the owners enjoyed these same tax benefits.)

Let's assume you own an investment property in which you originally invested $200,000 that is now worth $600,000. When you sell it, you may pay tax on the capital gain, possibly 15% of $400,000, or $60,000. This would leave you with proceeds of $540,000 to purchase a new property (assuming no debt).

If you sell this property and purchase another property

Section VI: Purchasing Property At Smith Mountain Lake

through a 1031 Exchange however, you would have the entire $600,000 available to purchase the new property. The tax on the gain would be deferred until the sale of that property in the future. The process could be repeated however, and the gain could be deferred indefinitely until the property is passed to your heirs. As I understand it, your heirs will actually get a new basis in the property, and the accumulated gains during your lifetime may *never be taxed*! (There may be limits on this.) Please consult an attorney and tax adviser to confirm how this may work in your situation.

Another possibility is for you to purchase an investment property through a 1031 Exchange and eventually (later) convert this property to your primary residence. In this case you could enjoy a gain of up to $500,000 tax-free on your residence, and switch the investment property, which was purchased with previously untaxed funds, over to your primary residence as well. Then this residence can also be sold with untaxed gains up to $500,000, according to tax accountants! Your original intent in the purchase of the investment property must be to use it for an investment purpose such as a vacation or long-term rental.

The like-kind requirement in a tax-deferred exchange is a frequently misunderstood element of this process. Some investors believe that the rules are strict, and one must swap a condo for a condo, or raw land for raw land. The rules, however, are actually broader than that according to most experts. You should be able to trade any investment real estate for any other. So you could sell an apartment building and replace it with a waterfront lot, or a condo for a waterfront home.

You should be aware that a 1031 Exchange requires an intermediary to handle the funds – you cannot touch the proceeds at all. You must also name a potential replacement property (or more than one) within 45 days, and close on a property(s) within 180 days. I work with an expert intermediary here in Virginia to whom I refer my clients.

The Definitive Guide to Smith Mountain Lake Real Estate

I once had a client who was selling an investment property and wanted to buy a waterfront lot and build an investment home with the 1031 proceeds. Since the builder could not guarantee that the home would be finished and closed on within 180 days, he hesitated. Through research, we learned that this was apparently possible, however, through a somewhat complex intermediate step with a third party set-up to take title to the land during the building process. This is an issue that should be discussed with a knowledgeable 1031 intermediary.

What if circumstances demand that you take title to a new property prior to the sale of your first property? Though this was not originally provided for in the 1031 regulations, this possibility apparently exists through IRS guidelines that were issued later. It is called a Reverse Exchange, and is more costly and difficult than a normal exchange. If tax savings are in the tens of thousands of dollars, however, it is often worth pursuing.

Since I think it unwise for me to delve further into tax advice, I would like to refer you to an excellent book on this subject: *How a Second Home Can Be Your Best Investment*, by Tom Kelly and John Tuccillo (McGraw Hill, 2004). You can order this book from Amazon.com. They do a great job with tax avoidance strategies as well as goal planning to make your second home dream a reality.

Equity Line of Credit
A great way to save a lot of money when buying a vacation home is to make an offer involving cash and a quick closing. I have seen sellers come off of their asking price more than I thought possible through using this strategy. One great way to finance this effort is to establish a home equity line of credit. This could provide you with immediate access to funds that would allow you to finance a home or lot until you get a longer-term loan, or you may decide to keep this financing arrangement long-term.

Section VI: Purchasing Property At Smith Mountain Lake

Seller Financing
Many owners at Smith Mountain Lake, like owners in other hot areas, have a lot of equity in their homes. They are also savvy investors. Some are open to the possibility of carrying a note in a second or third position that will allow you to purchase their lake home with little or no money down. I helped broker a deal like this earlier this year. A real estate agent will be able to assist you if you wish to place an offer and ask for partial or full owner financing.

Individual Retirement Account
Folks are surprised to learn that they can purchase a waterfront lot, home or condo within a self-directed Roth IRA. This government-blessed vehicle provides a great opportunity for you to own and enjoy your investment, and you can sell the property without tax within the IRA. (Be sure to check on occupancy rules since the property must be an investment property, not a primary residence, to my knowledge.) Also, the accumulated rents, proceeds, interest and appreciation can be withdrawn *with no tax consequence* after age 59½, from my understanding. This is because funds placed into a Roth IRA are placed into it with after-tax funds in the first place.

You can learn more about Roth IRAs from Equity Trust Company at **TrustETC.com**.

The Best Investment on Earth
Perhaps you have funds in money markets, CDs and stocks. You have seen the long-term graphs of the stock market's excellent performance over the last 100 years. However, I came to a point where I realized that I couldn't sip coffee and watch the sun rise from my mutual fund. The rising blip on my computer screen did not have a place for my son and me to throw in a fishing line. A number of years ago I cashed in most of my funds to invest in real estate. Everyone has only a short time on this earth to serve and love their family, and I want investments that I can personally enjoy *and* that will rise in

The Definitive Guide to Smith Mountain Lake Real Estate

value. Besides, have you seen the charts on real estate? I think it is the best investment available, and waterfront real estate makes it even more desirable. What about you? Are you ready to take the plunge? There's no better time than now! I hope to see you take the plunge here at Smith Mountain Lake!

Section VI: Purchasing Property At Smith Mountain Lake

Seller and Buyer Sittin' in a Tree...What is a Love Letter? Should I Write One? Why and How?

Back in the "good old days" of real estate (not so long ago...in the early 2000's in Northern Virginia and other areas), buyers were having a hard time purchasing the homes they wanted, or any home. Many buyers were beat out by other buyers again and again, even if their offer was submitted for full price or more on the first day the home was on the market.

After dealing with rejection over and over, some buyers came up with the idea of including a "love letter" with their offer. This is a letter that attempts to gain emotional support from the seller for this buyer. It paints a picture of how much the buyer likes the property and how they plan to enjoy it for years to come. Buyers often tell a story about their family, their children, their pets and why this is the perfect home for them. This strategy can also be used when offering a lower price or asking for furnishings.

The time is over when buyers made a list of insults to try to beat down sellers' prices. That never really worked anyway, in my opinion. It is a better strategy to compliment the seller on their good taste and give them a picture of how the next owner will enjoy the fruits of the sellers' labors and efforts.

Needless to say, I believe the love letter is a great relationship-building tool that buyers can use to help make their case to sellers. Even if there is not a competitive situation, it can help buyers make a connection with sellers that cannot come through a written offer alone.

One of my buyer couples simply did not quite have the financial ability to purchase the property of their dreams. Rather than give up on this lot, we worked with them to undertake this process. First, we did all of our due diligence upfront. We contacted a few builders to review the lot. We checked on all of the issues related to the dock and shoreline. We reviewed the lot with a surveyor and examined the septic permit on file with the county.

Second, we wrote up an offer. This offer was far below asking price, but was for cash and had no contingencies at all. The offer was right at the buyer's absolute financial limit. It included a large, non-refundable (if accepted) deposit check. Because we had done all of our due diligence upfront and had no contingencies, we had contacted a closing attorney and made a plan to close in 72 hours if the offer was accepted.

Third, the purchasers wrote a beautiful love letter. They told of their years of public service and their desire to retire at Smith Mountain Lake, the loveliest place they had ever seen. They told what type of home they planned to build and how their grandchildren would come to enjoy the lake.

Lastly, we contacted the seller's agent. She was surprised that we had already conducted the due diligence upfront, and even more surprised that we offered to close later that week. She shared, however, that the seller had previously declined offers higher than the one we were making.

The seller was a person of principle, and he cared about other factors in addition to the money. He therefore accepted the offer. He had never received an offer like this, and I think one of the deciding factors was the love letter. The seller felt a connection with the buyers and even asked if he could meet them. Even though the seller took far less than he desired, he felt great about the buyers and the transaction, and the buyers were able to acquire the property of their dreams.

Note that I am not recommending a manipulative strategy in which a buyer attempts to persuade a seller to do something that is not in his best interest. Rather I am suggesting a way for buyers to warm up the traditionally cold process of the written offer. The love letter takes what can sometimes be a frustrating and even insulting process and uses it to potentially form a bond between the parties. After all, the goal of a successful real estate transaction is a win-win. And maybe a few friendships can be developed along the way, which is a big plus in any transaction.

Section VI: Purchasing Property At Smith Mountain Lake

Do I Need a Home Inspection?

Q: Should I, as a buyer, get a home inspection?
A: YES!

Q: Are there situations where buyers, by their own choice, have opted to forego an official home inspection and as a result *saved tens of thousands of dollars*?
A: YES! However, I would need to qualify this response by explaining how they went about this. There is a creative way to get the benefit of a home inspection and still save *mucho dinero* on the purchase price. Using this technique gives some buyers the best of both worlds. This is situation-specific, so please contact me to get more information on how to accomplish it.

Q: Does the selection of a home inspector play an important role in the validity of the inspection's results, or do most inspectors perform the same investigations and come up with the same results?
A: The choice of a home inspector is important, especially if you are from outside of this area, and you choose a home inspector out of the phone book or without a personal recommendation. Many buyers are surprised to learn that home inspectors in Virginia have no significant license or experience requirements. It is possible that you could hire a home inspector who has few qualifications, little education, or no experience, yet has decided to be a home inspector.

A new friend called me in tears. She and her husband had relocated to Roanoke from Northern Virginia last year and made the mistake of not using a buyer's agent. When they placed an offer on a large home, they worked directly with the listing agent, and chose a home inspector out of the phone book. The inspector gave the home a virtually clean bill of health, and they made the purchase.

After months of suffering with wiring, plumbing and apparent structural problems, they called me for advice. The first thing they needed was an experienced, professional home inspector to undertake a thorough re-inspection. What this new inspector found horrified them. It appears that the house had been cobbled together in the builder-owner's spare time and had sat vacant and incomplete for more than 12 years in the process. Much of the home had apparently never been inspected (it was out in the country, deep in the woods!), and the wiring, plumbing, extensive decks, and much more needs a total overhaul. The cost of the repairs necessary just to get the home to a serviceable level will likely be $50,000 to $60,000.

There were many obvious things that were not built to code, which could have been a tip-off that there was something very wrong. Though no home inspector is perfect, if this couple had worked with a professional who represented their best interests, it is *probable* that their current suffering would have been avoided.

Lesson: Get personal recommendations and then obtain a home inspection from a professional, experienced home inspector.

PostScript: Few people are aware that there *may be* a way to file a claim through the title insurance company for some limited types of pre-existing damages. I helped my friends recover $25,000 of the damages that they suffered in the incident described above. Few homeowners have any idea that this option is available to them, but it can mean tens of thousands of dollars in recovered funds when unfortunate events occur. Talk to your closing attorney to see if this type of coverage is available through a premier title policy.

Q: Do I need a radon inspection for the home I am buying?
A: As in many places across the United States, some homes in this area have radon in the basement. While there does not seem to be more radon here than anywhere else, I strongly recommend that you conduct a radon test as part of the home-

Section VI: Purchasing Property At Smith Mountain Lake

buying process. The good news is that the fix for radon is always about the same and the cost is not that great. Typically, an agent can write up an offer that will compel the seller to pay for the cost of radon remediation prior to closing.

One note: There *may* be ways for a home seller to tamper with certain radon measurement devices. A smart home inspector with good equipment can detect this and frustrate their plans. Be sure to ask your inspector if he knows how to guard against this situation.

Do I Need a Property Survey?

When purchasing property with an existing home at Smith Mountain Lake, you may not always need a new survey. Using an existing survey is often considered sufficient and could save you hundreds of dollars. Examine the existing survey closely however, to make sure that the buildings and lot lines seem to be in order. If you are even the least bit unsure, get a survey, or at least get professional advice!

If you are building a home, dock, shed, garage, or cutting trees anywhere near your property line, you need to know where the boundaries are and what setback rules are in effect for construction. If the lines are not clearly marked, it would probably be wise to get a new survey or at least have the boundaries marked off.

I know of a man who bought a lot and was building a home in the northern part of the lake. He was reportedly trying to save $400 by not surveying the new home on the lot. In his mind the home site was clearly nowhere near the lot lines. Unfortunately, he had a mistaken assumption about the boundaries of the lot when he purchased it. Though he thought he was building in the middle of his lot, he actually built over the neighbor's property line. This caused quite a problem, and both parties later became belligerent. As a result, the construction on his home was held up for a year or more while this was resolved. Please don't make this mistake!

Another friend of mine recently received a call from his neighbor and was told that some of his landscaping, including part of his sprinkler system, was on the neighbor's lot. This neighbor had done a survey and the boundary line was not where my friend had always thought it was. He is now hiring his own surveyor to confirm this.

Your real estate agent should be able to provide you with a county GIS survey and a plat for the property you plan to purchase. If no plat can be obtained and you have any questions about the property line or setbacks, the REALTOR® can assist you

Section VI: Purchasing Property At Smith Mountain Lake

in taking appropriate steps. This may include asking for a survey as a condition to purchase the property.

Note that in addition to a survey, it is also important to know what easements the property you are purchasing is granting to neighbors, power companies or others. A property survey is *not* necessarily the best place to find this information. You need to examine your deed to see what easements have been granted to others and what other easements that your property benefits from as well. If you have any questions on these items, you should ask your closing attorney.

I Want to Buy a Home at the Lake, but I Dread Paying for Flood Insurance. Will I Need it?

Many buyers (and even mortgage companies from outside the lake area) assume that waterfront homeowners here need costly flood insurance. This is rarely the case. In fact, I can recall only one situation that I was involved with in which a waterfront homeowner required flood insurance, and that was debatable.

Flood insurance is required when all or part of a home is within the 100-year flood plain. This area is defined up to the point of 803 feet above sea level. This is eight vertical feet above the full lake level of 795 feet above sea level. This point will vary widely depending on the slope of the lot. On a steep lot, it may be only 10 to 20 feet from the shoreline, while on a flatter lot it could be a significant distance back from the water.

Appalachian Power Company (APCO) does a wonderful job controlling the lake level, and has controls in place that do not allow the lake to rise above its normal level except in extreme circumstances. I don't know of a time when the lake level has risen above the 100-year floodplain area.

Section VI: Purchasing Property At Smith Mountain Lake

How is the Dock Transferred to the New Owner at Closing?

Appalachian Power has dock transfer guidelines and procedures that have a significant impact on the sale of Smith Mountain Lake real estate. These guidelines result in responsibility and liability on all parties involved in selling and buying waterfront property here. The goal of these guidelines is to ensure that boat docks are in compliance with APCO regulations.

Under these guidelines, the power company processes the transfer of the dock permit (if applicable) separately from the closing of the real estate itself. Though the dock or boathouse is owned by the property owner, it is technically on property that is managed by the power company (the lake).

The power company wants to be sure that no significant changes to the structure have been made by the property owner since the dock was last inspected. If the dock was originally constructed under a permit, it should have been inspected at that time. Typically, there would have been no reason to inspect the structure since. If the dock is now inspected as part of the transfer, and it is discovered that changes have been made that render it currently non-compliant, the power company may choose to not transfer the dock (usage) permit until the issues are resolved.

How could this play out as a practical matter? Let's say that the owner of a property with a permitted dock decides to add a floater to their dock without obtaining a new permit. Assuming this floater would not violate the current size limit or setback requirements, according to my understanding, if APCO discovers this when they inspect the dock for the transfer, they would likely make the owner apply for a permit and have it approved prior to allowing the dock permit transfer. If it violates the current size or setback limits, the floater would not be permitted and it would need to be dismantled prior to APCO transferring the dock occupancy and use permit to the new owner.

For example, let's say the owner of a dock with an original enclosed room of 70 square feet expanded the room by 30 square feet without a permit. In this case, since the total enclosed area is now out of compliance with current regulations, the power company could force the owner to dismantle the additional area to bring the dock back into compliance before transferring the permit to the new owner.

At the risk of sounding self-serving (surely you'd never accuse me of that would you?), this is another significant reason I highly recommend that you select a professional real estate agent to assist you in the purchase (or sale) of your Smith Mountain Lake home. This is one of those issues that never come up in a typical For Sale By Owner in your neighborhood, and the REALTORS® here have typically become experts in this arena.

If you need more information or are unsure how these issues will play out in your situation, consult your real estate professional or contact APCO at (540) 985-2579 or email them at aepsmp@aep.com.

To obtain a copy of the regulations for building a dock, see the Shoreline Management Plan, which is available at **http://www.smithmtn.com.**

Section VI: Purchasing Property At Smith Mountain Lake

How Do I Close on My Smith Mountain Lake Property?

So you've struck a deal on the perfect, once-in-a-lifetime waterfront property! How do you go from there to getting the deed in hand? What will it cost to close on your property? By now you know the first thing I am going to say: Let your real estate professional guide you from this point, as s/he has through the entire process.

Inspections

There are a number of inspections to be performed in the process of transferring a home here. The seller is typically required to fund and conduct three inspections within less than 30 days of closing. The first is a termite inspection. The seller will hire an inspector to examine the home for evidence of wood boring insects.

The seller is also responsible to conduct a test of the well water (assuming the home is on a private well). This is a simple test to check for bacteria in the water, not an extensive test of water quality.

The seller will also conduct an inspection to ensure the proper operation of the septic system (assuming the home is not on a community or public sewer). Often the same inspector will conduct all three tests. If evidence of any problem from these inspections is discovered, the seller, unless otherwise agreed upon in the contract, is responsible to correct this situation in order to proceed to closing.

As I mentioned earlier, you as a purchaser may also choose to have a home inspection and a radon inspection. In addition, you may choose to request a more extensive water report and septic inspection. I have had purchasers ask for each of these. The septic inspection may include a visual inspection of the tank using a special camera. Sometimes an older tank may become corroded and need to be repaired or replaced. The basic required inspection will not find this defect, but it would need to be repaired if you are going to rent your home in Bedford County. A more extensive water test may include testing the water for other "less harmful" substances that you may choose to have filtered out of your water. If you plan to consider asking the seller to pay for repairs from these two inspections, or if you would consider calling off the purchase for bad results, be sure to delineate these terms carefully in the contract upfront.

The Closing Agent
In Virginia, the purchaser has the right to select the closing agent. Closings are typically conducted by a closing attorney or a title company. This agent coordinates the various elements of the closing including the title examination, deed preparation, prior mortgage (deed of trust) payoff, the new mortgage, title insurance, allocation for property taxes and homeowner dues, recording of the deed and mortgage, payment of recording fees, transfer tax payments, and the payment of any fees for services including realty commissions and inspections or other liens not paid previously. The closing agent summarizes all of these charges and allocations on the closing statement. You should request an advance copy of the closing statement prior to closing to ask any questions, look for any errors, and to avoid needless delays on closing day.

The Deed
It is extremely important for you to examine your deed when purchasing property anywhere. The deed is the ownership title for the property and the definitive document for many rights and encumbrances of the property. These may include power company easements, easements previously granted to neighbors, rights for common areas such as boat launches, requirements to adhere to neighborhood restrictions, and much more.
   We worked with a seller who was using a deed that detailed the rules for constructing a dock in that neighborhood, which is

Section VI: Purchasing Property At Smith Mountain Lake

unusual. Upon examining the deed, the buyer discovered that the current owner had built his dock too far into the cove. That meant that the seller was faced with obtaining a variance on his existing dock from the neighborhood property owner's association before he could sell his home. By examining the deed, the purchaser saved himself from inheriting this potentially nasty problem.

Talk to your closing attorney about examining your deed before purchasing your new property.

Closing Long Distance
These days, many closings are handled long distance without either party coming to town on the day of closing. If this is best for you, the closing attorney and realty agents can use email, fax, overnight mail, and wire transfer. This will save you a drive to the lake, although the main downside is that you may not have the opportunity to do a walk-through of the property just prior to closing. Talk to your realty agent about how to best manage this situation.

Closing Costs
Though each situation is different, the following is a list of *typical* closing costs for a transaction in this region of Virginia at the time of this writing.

Purchaser Closing Costs

Title Examination	$100
Closing Attorney Fees	$350 to $450
Deed Recording Fee (transfer tax)	0.33% x price
Mortgage (Deed of Trust) Recording Fee	0.317% x loan amt
Mortgage Points and Other Charges	Variable
Property Taxes*	Pro-rated
Homeowner Association Dues*	Pro-rated if any
Title Insurance**	Up to 0.4% x price
Deed Recording Fee	$33
Mortgage (Deed of Trust) Recording Fee	$46
Realty Commissions	$0***

* Property tax and homeowner association dues may be owed to you by the seller – or owed by you to the seller – depending on who is paying the actual bill and when.

**Note that title insurance is not legally required for cash purchases in Virginia, but it is *highly recommended.* Mortgage companies always require you to purchase title insurance to cover their interests. Talk to your closing agent for more information.

*** While it is common for purchasers here to pay nothing in realty commissions, it is illegal for multiple companies in a market to jointly establish realty commission rates. Commission rates here average about the same as other markets in the United States. Talk to your realty professional for more information.

Seller Closing Costs

Deed preparation	$100
Grantor (transfer) tax	0.1% x price
Property Taxes*	Pro-rated
Homeowner Association Dues	Pro-rated if any
Realty Commissions**	As Negotiated

* Property tax and homeowner association dues may be owed to you by the purchaser – or owed by you to the purchaser – depending on who is paying the actual bill and when.

** It is illegal for multiple companies in a market to jointly establish realty commission rates. Commission rates here average about the same as other markets in the United States. Talk to your realty professional for more information.

One final note: As a home seller or purchaser, you may wish to purchase a home warranty. This will warrant a large number of home elements for the purchaser for at least a year after closing. This may allay the purchaser's fears of problems and could help

Section VI: Purchasing Property At Smith Mountain Lake

avoid tensions between the parties after closing. These warranties typically cost between $350 and $450 for one year.

Section VII:
Choosing a REALTOR® at Smith Mountain Lake

What's in This Section?

Do I Really Need a REALTOR® to Acquire my SML Dream Home?

Choosing a REALTOR® for Your SML Transaction

Choosing a Buyer's Agent at Smith Mountain Lake

Selling Your Home? Special Considerations in Selecting a Listing Agent at Smith Mountain Lake

The Definitive Guide to Smith Mountain Lake Real Estate

Do I Really Need a REALTOR® to Acquire my SML Dream Home?

As you've probably noticed, the real estate world has graduated to the era of big data. From the comfort of your recliner, you can view data on virtually any house, condo or lot in any corner of the world. You can drive down virtual streets and nearly peek in the windows of most any home on the planet. You can collect reams of electronic data from multiple sources showing floor plans, tax values, ownership and sale data till your head spins. Zillow's® massive supercomputers in Irvine, CA will even calculate what they believe you should offer and pay for most properties.

But your dream home is more than a collection of data! So much more than zeros and ones in the cloud.

Though I see the value of *big data* in many typical neighborhood settings, where home styles, lots, views and sizes are somewhat homogenous, *this approach simply will not fly in a mountain-lake resort setting.*
Big Data alone could lead to a big mistake. And a lot of heartache. You really need a local SML real estate agent to help you locate and acquire your dream home at Smith Mountain Lake.
Top real estate agents here know the value of every one of the 2,724,800 feet (yes, that's 520 miles) of shoreline here at Smith Mountain Lake. Agents here have intimate knowledge of every cove and every channel... the views and slopes and home styles that grace our lovely mountain shores.

Did you hear about the Zillow CEO's home sale?
Zillow has become nationally famous for bringing automated property valuation technology to the real estate world. Zillow's infamous ***Zestimates*** allow buyers and sellers to estimate the

Section VII: Choosing a REALTOR® at Smith Mountain Lake

value of the home they plan to buy or sell.

So how did Zillow's automated technology (*Zestimates*) perform when Zillow's CEO, Spencer Rascoff, sold his own home back in early 2016?

It missed the mark by a whopping 70%!

A screenshot showing Zillow's estimate of Rascoff's home the day after it sold for $1.05 million showed its Zestimate at $1,750,405. *Zillow over-Zestimated their CEO's home by over 70%!*

When questioned about the discrepancy, Zillow acknowledged what we all know intuitively: Automated Valuation Models cannot account for subjective differences in houses. *Houses are not commodities.*

While this is true in general, it is even more true for luxury homes.

In commenting on this embarrassing event, Zillow Senior Economist Skylar Olsen said that the Zestimate of Rascoff's home represents "the classic luxury homes problem. Zestimates can't take into account 'non-quantifiable facts,' such as layout design or lighting, and these facts can have much more of an effect on the values of luxury homes than less expensive properties," she said.

While every intelligent buyer and seller intuitively knows this is true, everyone still wants to believe "the facts" when they work to their benefit. So sellers hope higher values are correct, while buyers look for lower values to support their desire to get a fair deal. It can cause a real problem, especially for buyers who aren't familiar with the area, or who don't have a trusted local expert to assist them.

While luxury homes present a valuation challenge, luxury homes at a mountain lake complicate the matter even further.

After reading the Zillow story in the news, I decided to do a little research of my own. In my brief research of recent local SML waterfront home sales, I found that high Zestimates outnumbered low ones by a wide margin. Perhaps by over four-to-one in the window of time I reviewed.

Now if you were an SML buyer, and you were just relying on these Zestimates, you could get burned. (Of course *you* would never do that. The fact that you're reading this book proves that.)

But you may wonder how you can get a handle on waterfront property values at Smith Mountain Lake. Like I said, if Zillow can't get luxury home prices right in town, the complications caused at a mountain lake resort make it a sheer impossibility.

Knowledge is *NOT* necessarily power

Quoting broker associate and REALTOR® Cara Ameer (*10 Reasons you should never buy or sell without an agent.* Inman News June 16, 2016):

> Knowledge is not power. A little knowledge can be a dangerous thing when it comes to real estate. At the click of a mouse or a tap on your phone, you can get an instant valuation of your property.
>
> Is that value realistic? On which properties is it based? What did those properties have that yours does or does not? What were the dates and details of those sales?
>
> That valuation could be significantly more or less than what your property is actually worth. Just like using the internet to self-diagnose a medical issue is not the best idea, the same applies to real estate. **A little knowledge can be a dangerous thing when it comes to real estate.**

Section VII: Choosing a REALTOR® at Smith Mountain Lake

In the second section of this book, I cover the seven unique factors that drive Smith Mountain Lake property values. An experienced SML real estate agent knows these factors well, and event if you have personal experience in real estate in other geographic areas, you would do well to acquire a great agent here at the lake before starting on your quest to acquire your dream home.

Choosing a REALTOR® for Your SML Transaction

As I've stated earlier, if you're considering purchasing or selling a property at Smith Mountain Lake, it is *critical* that you hire a real estate professional. Why do you need representation? And how do you choose the right REALTOR® to represent you?

Representation

Can you imagine going on trial without hiring an attorney? Sure, you could do it, but how wise would it be to entrust yourself to your own limited knowledge? If you agree, why would you take a risk with one of your largest and most important investments?

If you already have a specific property in mind when you decide to hire a realty agent, it may not be wise to hire the agent who represents the property you are interested in purchasing. Continuing the analogy, if you were on trial, can you imagine hiring the opposing attorney to represent you as well? There are many instances where this would not cause you harm, but generally it is best to seek out your own agent. With this in mind, let's discuss how to find the best agent at Smith Mountain Lake.

National REALTOR® Statistics

Here are some stats to consider when selecting an agent. According to the National Association of REALTORS® 2015 survey, agents' median income was $45,800. Licensed brokers earned a median income of $65,300, while sales agents earned $33,900. Approximately 42% of REALTORS® with two years of experience or less grossed under $10,000. More than 25% of all REALTORS® have earned a bachelor's degree and 10% of agents have graduate degrees.

There are many variables when choosing an agent. None of the statistics above will determine whether you will get a good or bad agent, but it is important that you don't automatically choose the first agent you speak with or pick one out of the

Section VII: Choosing a REALTOR® at Smith Mountain Lake

phonebook. Interview them and test them out. Let's consider this further in the next section.

Choosing a Buyer's Agent at Smith Mountain Lake

I hope you now realize that you face complex issues when purchasing waterfront property here at Smith Mountain Lake. Unless you already live on the lake and are intimately familiar with all of these issues, it is *crucial* that you locate an agent who will work to find the best property for you *and* assure that you avoid the pitfalls enumerated here. How do you find an agent like this?

First of all, I believe it is important that you select a full-time agent -- someone whose family is depending on this individual to earn the income needed to survive. As you can see from the statistics above, many agents are not full-time. I can tell you from experience as a full-time buyer's agent that it is challenging to stay on top of all of the listings available out there. When you contact a buyer's agent looking for a certain type of property, it is imperative that they have a working knowledge of the inside and the outside of a large variety of homes on the market. It is difficult for a part-timer to do this.

Second, you should attempt to work with a seasoned Smith Mountain Lake agent. The growing popularity of Smith Mountain Lake has drawn many new realty agents and investors, so it is important that you ask a prospective agent about their experience and credentials.

Third, you should select an agent who is fully devoted to Smith Mountain Lake, not an agent who works in a nearby city and is only slightly familiar with the lake. There are fantastic agents in nearby areas, but they are often not aware of the variety and complexity of issues involved in the purchase of real estate here at Smith Mountain Lake.

Thanks to the Multiple Listing Service (MLS) of the local Board of REALTORS®, any licensed realty agent can arrange a showing on any property on the market, regardless of who has it listed. Many clients often get a sneak peak at "pocket listings" that have not yet been formally listed.

Section VII: Choosing a REALTOR® at Smith Mountain Lake

SML buyer agents must be able to assist clients in knowing the waterfront situation at a variety of properties. With all of the online resources available to the public today, it is critical that agents be able to quickly comment on a variety of prospective listings that a client selects online. When a client calls and tells me he has found the perfect property online, I can virtually guarantee that it will *not* be the property he selects when he comes to town. It almost never fails. There are just too many factors that are hard to capture in a description, photo and virtual tour. This is partly what makes SML such a unique and wonderful place. However, it also means that you need a devoted agent to help sort out these factors.

As an example, once a client of a newer realty team member selected about 10 homes that interested him. One of our veteran team members, and one of the top buyer agents at Smith Mountain Lake, went down the list and was able to comment in detail on each of these homes. His analysis included a description of the lot, the view, the slope, the neighborhood, and in some cases the rental potential for the home. All from memory. This is invaluable information that you would normally not receive from a part-time or inexperienced agent. Choose a devoted Smith Mountain Lake agent. Don't be afraid to ask tough questions, and if you don't get the answers you want, don't fear politely excusing yourself from the relationship. There is too much at stake to leave it in the hands of a rookie.

One if by Land, Two if by Sea
Since you are likely coming to Smith Mountain Lake for the lake and the mountains, it probably makes sense to see properties both by car and by boat. Strangely enough, they are quite different and it is important to get both views, at least when you are in the process of narrowing down the field to the top candidates. I have seen a number of occasions where someone really liked a property when arriving through the front

door, but was scared away when they got there via the dock. Or vice-versa. You may even want to see an aerial view of your top picks. I had a client searching for lots a few years back who elected to see his top picks by boat and from the air in a private plane. This gave us a unique perspective and gave the buyer great confidence in purchasing his expensive dream property.

Since many of the lake agents live at or near the water, there are many who routinely show property by boat. It is really worth the effort to do both if you can.

Do a Trial Run
If you have interviewed a few buyer (or listing) agents and you think you've located the right one for you, give them a test before making a commitment. Ask them to investigate a number of issues for you with an agreed upon deadline. This could be as simple as pulling listings for a number of properties meeting certain criteria. Then privately hold them accountable to getting the information back to you in a timely and professional fashion. If they don't perform as planned, it may be the signal for you to find another agent. If you are unsure after the first trial, give them a tougher one and see how it goes. I am sad to say that some realty agents do not always follow through on their commitments. You should not have to bear the consequences of their laziness in the process of acquiring or selling one of your largest assets.

Section VII: Choosing a REALTOR® at Smith Mountain Lake

Selling Your Home? Special Considerations in Selecting a Listing Agent at Smith Mountain Lake

Smith Mountain Lake is a unique place, far from most of its buyers. This means that if you are a seller, it is important that you choose an agent that will market your property in the most effective manner possible. Here are some things to consider and questions to ask your prospective listing agent.

Full-time, Experienced, and Lake-Centric
As I mentioned before, it is critical that you choose a listing agent who is full-time, honest, experienced, and committed to Smith Mountain Lake. You cannot afford to misprice your home either too high or low, and it just doesn't make sense to sell yourself short by hiring anything less than a top professional.

I know of at least two sellers who were the victims of under-pricing by their listing agent. This cost each of them more than $100,000 as well as much bitter grief when multiple offers came in during the first two days of their listing period.

Conversely, there is no shortage of overpriced homes in this market, as in every market. This typically does the seller no favors either, as the listing often gets stale and is overlooked even after the price is appropriately dropped.

It is often challenging to properly price real estate here at the lake. The wide variety of factors makes it utterly unlike homes in the city, where a general homogeneity allows agents to estimate the price of some homes over the phone based on the address and description.

Marketing Plan
What type of marketing plan does the agent have for your property? You want to be sure not to hire an agent that only uses the Three-P Marketing Plan: (1) **P**lace a sign in your yard; (2) **P**ut it in the MLS; and (3) **P**ray that it sells! Marketing a property in these times should be much more involved than this.

There are many factors involved in properly marketing a property here at Smith Mountain Lake. Ask your prospective listing agent for his marketing plan for your property. In addition to reviewing the subjective aspects of an agent's marketing plan, there is a way to objectively gauge the effectiveness of their program. The National Association of REALTORS® says that only about 15% of listings are sold by the listing agent for that property. So about 85% of the properties are sold through the effectiveness of the Multiple Listing Service (MLS) and the listing agent's networking ability with other agents. The 15% of sales that are made by the listing agent typically represent calls made on the yard sign and the balance of the listing agent's marketing program aimed at obtaining buyers for a specific property. So if you want to gauge the effectiveness of a listing agent's marketing campaign, ask them what percentage of their listings are sold by them or their team of buyer agents. And ask them to show you the statistics. If they say about 15%, their program is probably about average. If you want an agent with an above-average program, you should look for an agent with a higher percentage. If the agent has no idea, that is probably not a great sign.

Staging Your Home
In addition to great marketing and accurate pricing, I believe that staging your home is the third most important factor in selling it. In Great Britain they call it "House Doctoring." Home staging is the process of preparing your home before it goes up for sale. The goal is to sell a home quickly and for the most money possible by attracting the highest number of potential buyers. Staging transforms a property into a welcoming, appealing, and attractive product. It raises the value of a property by making it less cluttered, cleaner and better landscaped. For vacant homes, rental furniture can be used to create a living space in which buyers can imagine themselves living. Properly executed staging leads the eye to attractive features and minimizes flaws.

Section VII: Choosing a REALTOR® at Smith Mountain Lake

Staging a home to show well and sell is important in any market, but it is most critical in a buyer's market. If a prospective home buyer is looking at 10 properties in your price range on a given day, you need to do everything you can as a seller to be certain your property is at or near the top of their list of favorites. In a buyer's market, make it your goal to have your home in the top $1/3^{rd}$ in terms of staging and condition, and in the bottom $1/3^{rd}$ of pricing – compared to similar homes in the market.

One of my Smith Mountain Homes team members recently sold a home that had been sitting on the market for about a year. The home was vacant, and had showed so-so for most of its time on the market. These buyers chose it over all of the other homes they toured that day, however, and they wrote an offer right away. What had changed? The owner hired a home stager who completed her work two weeks beforehand. The efforts of the stager made a difference, as attested to by the quick sale of the property.

I have been using a home stager to help market my listings for some time, and recommend that you do the same. If you are selling a home in the Smith Mountain Lake area, there are a number of professional home stagers to choose from. Make sure to get a recommendation and references, and see some of their recent work before hiring one for your property.

Note that if you are selling a vacant building lot, you should still be thinking about staging. Ask yourself and others what you can do to make your lot show as well as possible. This will often include marking the property lines carefully, trimming trees to open up the view near the water, clearing brush throughout the lot, and even constructing a path.

I'm happy to recommend my home stager to anyone who contacts me. She is world class, and increases the value on each home she stages by a wide margin. She staged two homes for me recently, and both received multiple offers in a short time. Interestingly, both were listed for about 10% to 15% more than I had planned... before her staging. Do the math. She may not be immediately available, and she will not be cheap, but if you would like to talk to her, please contact me at **paul.moore@SmithMountainHomes.com**.

MLS Listing Presentation

There is an art to the wording and photography on an MLS listing. The agent should give thought and effort to the preparation of the listing. It should not be just a simple recitation of the facts, but it should paint a picture for the prospective buyer and other lake agents.

The photography for the agent's listings should be professional level. It is *critical* that the main photo for your property be carefully thought through by the agent. It must put your property in the best possible light. This is crucial when marketing your listing to other agents as well as the vast online public.

I've recently started doing split-photos for the main photo. I splice together four different views of the property. This is especially effective for a home that has a beautifully staged interior and great views. Your agent may choose to use one exterior shot, a kitchen shot, a bathroom or bedroom photo, and a photo showing the lake or mountain view. The last five homes I've listed used this style for the main photo, and four of them got a lot of attention and offers.

A buyer's agent has only so much time to investigate, preview, and show properties to a prospective buyer. You need to be sure that your property, if possible, is on the agent's short list of properties in your price range. A perfect example occurred a few summers back. There was a particular home that had never made my short list of homes to show buyers. I could not pinpoint a particular reason other than the fact that the fuzzy, distant picture gave me a bad impression of it. The description did it no favors, either. There were many homes on the market, and I hadn't talked to another agent who had shown it or could even remember it. Somehow my clients ended up choosing it as part of their list of 10 homes to see one Sunday

Section VII: Choosing a REALTOR® at Smith Mountain Lake

afternoon. We pulled up to the dock to the most pleasant of surprises. It was a charming cottage on a beautiful lot. It had a wide water sunset view and everything else my client wanted. They put in an offer that evening and moved in a month later. I think it would have been sold several times over if the main photo and description had shown it as it really was. The buyers were thrilled, and in this case I had to give them all the credit since they picked it in spite of the photo. (Maybe they really didn't need a REALTOR® after all! ☺)

If you are interviewing listing agents, ask them to send along their other listings. Review them thoroughly to ensure that they are taking the care necessary in both wording and photography for each of their listings.

Selling Your Property *Twice*
If your listing agent is doing his job, he will have a plan to sell your property twice – first to the other lake agents and second to the actual buyer. Generally, as discussed above, there is about an 85% chance that your property will be sold by another agent in the local MLS area. For this reason, it is imperative that your listing agent has a clear focus on marketing your property to the other agents. This could take place through well-designed email blasts announcing your listing and later price changes, an invitation for agents to view the listing on their website, REALTOR® open houses, and a well-designed MLS presentation, as discussed above. Then it must be well-marketed to the general public as well. If you sense that an agent doesn't have a deep desire to market your property to other agents first, you may wonder if the agent is hoping to sell the property directly to one of his clients. Which may reduce your buyer pool and net sale price. You may then wonder if the agent is really working for your best interests or his own. I rarely find this among Smith Mountain Lake agents, but I imagine that it happens. Don't underestimate the importance of this issue in choosing a listing agent.

Multi-Agent Opinion – Four Eyes are Better than Two

There are probably many agents who successfully price properties without a second agent's opinion. I, for one, don't do this. I believe the pricing of your property is too important to be done solo.

My team believes that it is important to give two or three agents a tour of the property before making a decision. Our agents each go back and review comparable properties independently in order to determine an estimated list price for the home. We each offer our price opinion and then defend our position to the other agents. We virtually always end up agreeing on a list price, and this is the figure we recommend to our clients.

I don't think this is the only way to price a property, but it is the way I am most comfortable with. If you agree, you may wish to ask your listing agent to take a similar approach.

Website Design

A listing agent should have, or have access to, a fantastic website. It should present the lake, the agent, and your property in the most favorable possible light. It should offer the online user many options to get more information on the lake. It should be a pleasant and informative site that users bookmark to return to when they're thinking about waterfront living.

Website Advertising. "If you build it – they *won't* come"

One can't just put up a website and hope people will come. The site must be aggressively advertised on Google, Yahoo, and other major search engines. This is an art and a science of its own, and it needs a focused, strategic effort on the part of the listing agent or his team. What keyword search terms point to this website? Prospective SML buyers are not usually searching under generic terms such as Keller Williams Realty or Wainwright & Company. Think about how you would search if you were a potential buyer. Then perform these searches and see whose sites are coming up in the ads in the first few pages.

Section VII: Choosing a REALTOR® at Smith Mountain Lake

These are the agents that are investing the money to ensure that their listings are being seen by hundreds of people online daily. More than 90% of SML buyers are searching for property on the web, so your listing agent better be there in a big way.

Website Search Engine Placement
In addition to website advertising, a good listing website will have good search engine placement. This indicates that the programmers and site reviewers at Google, Yahoo and elsewhere have determined by the keywords being used that this site is relevant to the needs of those who are searching. Here's what I mean. When someone does a Google search, they don't know what specific sites they want to access (if they did, they could just type the site name into the address line). It is Google's job to raise the most relevant websites to the top of the search rankings so users will get to these relevant sites. This is how Google became a household word (even a verb!) in the last 15 years.

If you type in search terms that are likely to be typed in by someone looking for a property like yours, your listing agent's website will likely come up near the top of the search. It is unlikely that a buyer would type in a specific search phrase (like Smith Mountain Lake Home Waverly Subdivision), though it is possible in some cases. It is more likely that a buyer would type in "Smith Mountain Lake VA Home" or "Smith Mountain Lake Real Estate."

This is a critical issue because it is important for buyers to see your listing prominently displayed when they are searching for a property. It is also important because it is an indicator of how much effort your listing agent is making to promote your home.

In addition to searching these terms yourself, ask your agent what effort he or she is making to continually improve his site's search engine ranking. This is referred to as Search Engine Optimization (SEO). There are many components of a typical SEO strategy, including keyword optimization, content creation and earning links from relevant websites and blogs utilizing various strategies, techniques and tactics. Many real estate agents sponsor their own blogs as well. This is an effective way to promote a geographic area and to advertise new properties that come on the market.

Section VIII:
Smith Mountain Lake – A Great Place to Own Real Estate!

What's in This Section?

What Amenities, Accommodations & Entertainment Does Smith Mountain Lake Offer?

How Does the Cost of Living Compare to Other Areas of the United States?

How is the Weather at Smith Mountain Lake? Do You Have Hurricanes Like Other Waterfront Destinations?

I Love to Sail or Want to Learn. Are there Areas of the Lake that are Better for Sailing?

Is There a Warm Side Versus a Cold Side of this Lake?

How Could Global Warming Affect Vacation Properties in the U.S.? How Will this Affect Smith Mountain Lake?

Is Smith Mountain Lake a Profitable Place to Invest?

Smith Mountain Lake Versus the Beach

Come to the Mountains…

What Amenities, Accommodations & Entertainment Does Smith Mountain Lake Offer?

Smith Mountain Lake is attracting many new buyers from other lakes. We regularly hear about the lack of amenities at Lake Anna, Gaston, Kerr, and other lakes. Apparently Lake Anna has only a few restaurants, for example. We have a number of buyers who drive twice as far to get to Smith Mountain Lake rather than Lake Anna.

Smith Mountain Lake is unique due to our quiet, rural lifestyle and the amenities of a larger resort. Just last year, a number of new restaurants opened, and many more are planned and under construction. There are marinas, hotels, and building supply centers already here. We also have a small airport, which has been an excellent way for our clients to get to the lake to tour property on short notice. To get a better picture of Smith Mountain Lake's amenities, visit my news and information site at **SmithMountainHomes.com/News**. This site features retail and commercial amenities around the lake and is a great resource for things you may need when you plan your next visit. Also try **VisitSmithMountainLake.com**, the site for the Smith Mountain Lake Chamber of Commerce.

Here is a list of some local amenities and entertainment at Smith Mountain Lake and the surrounding region:

- Dozens of restaurants, including several on the waterfront
- Various bars and grilles, including some on the waterfront
- Many hotels, including several waterfront
- Several local Bed & Breakfasts
- About 20 waterfront marinas as well as some local off-water boat centers
- Boat and jet ski rentals
- One of the top (the top?) waterfront state parks in the nation
- Various camping, hiking and sightseeing opportunities
- Houseboat rentals (USA Today says SML is one of the top

Section VIII: SML – A Great Place to Own Real Estate!

10 places in the nation to float a houseboat -- 3rd to be exact)
- Booker T. Washington National Monument
- The Blue Ridge Parkway
- The National D-Day Memorial
- Several colleges within an hour
- Churches of many denominations
- The Blue Ridge Farm Institute and Museum
- The Crooked Road Music Trail
- Five golf courses (including one of the top ranked in the Eastern United States)
- Smith Mountain Lake "Virginia Dare" Dinner Cruise
- Various horseback riding and boarding stables
- Poplar Forest, Thomas Jefferson's summer home
- SML Dam & Visitor Center
- Drive-in Theatre
- A 4-plex movie theater
- Many historical sites including Civil War battlefields
- Helicopter tours
- Two YMCAs
- Curves exercise facility
- Several vineyards and wineries
- Pick 'em yourself blueberry & blackberry orchards
- Three large building supply centers
- Two national grocery stores and many family-owned markets
- Several putt-putt golf courses
- Blue Ridge Dinner Theatre
- Several art galleries
- Campgrounds and camper sites
- Waterfront cabin rental community
- Local medical facilities and several major hospitals nearby
- Various sport fishing outfitters
- Airport two minutes from the lake

- Wakeboard and skate shop
- Various furniture and other interior design stores
- Smith Mountain Lake Sailing School
- State of the art library
- Top deer population in Virginia (Bedford County – great for hunters… and nature loving vegetarians alike!)
- Too many amenities to mention in nearby Roanoke, Lynchburg, Charlottesville, Raleigh and Greensboro
- …And so much more!

Medical Facilities
Smith Mountain Lake's serenity and mountain location may cause some to be concerned about the adequacy and proximity of medical facilities in the area. Roanoke's Carilion Hospital, less than an hour away, has a top-notch trauma center, and Lynchburg has Centra, a similar caliber hospital system, also about an hour away. A short helicopter ride in an emergency.

We have a variety of other medical facilities around the lake. Here is a list:

- Carilion Velocity Care
- Carilion Internal Medicine
- Carilion Cardiology Clinic
- Carilion Orthopaedic Surgery
- Connect Hearing
- Home Instead Senior Care
- Physicians to Children
- Ridge View Dermatology
- Runk & Pratt Residential Adult Care
- Vistar Eye Center

Section VIII: SML – A Great Place to Own Real Estate!

How Does the Cost of Living Compare to Other Areas of the United States?

I have been shamelessly bragging about the many benefits we Smith Mountain Lakers enjoy that are foreign to many oceanfront and other resort communities. Another feature we enjoy here is a lower cost of living.

I used to live in Metro Detroit, and I can tell you that in my experience, and in the experience of many others who come here, the lifestyle costs are low. Gasoline is less expensive here than anywhere I have traveled. The cost of building a new home happily shocked my recent buyer from the West Coast. Food is lower. The slower pace here also seems to encourage my family to somehow spend less. I know that we were eating out far more often in Detroit, and I have to say that I am thoroughly enjoying my wife's home cooked meals here far more than those of any city restaurant. Yet we happily have those options also. Some of the best restaurants in Southwest Virginia are right here at Smith Mountain Lake!

One major factor in the decreased cost of living is the low tax rates. I don't know about taxes where you live, but my clients from Northern Virginia, Pennsylvania, New Jersey California, New York and many other places are stunned to find out how low their property taxes are here compared to back home. One of my clients planning to move here from a waterfront home in the Finger Lakes region of upstate New York tells me that his home there is costing him more than $12,000 in annual taxes. A similarly priced home here will probably cost him about $3,500 for annual taxes.

If you want to find out how taxes and other costs of living compare to your area, visit some of our home listings at **SmithMountainHomes.com**, or contact us by phone or email.

How is the Weather at Smith Mountain Lake? Do You Have Hurricanes Like Other Waterfront Destinations?

One of the great benefits to owning a home at Smith Mountain Lake is a lack of bad weather. The lake is far enough inland from hurricane areas near the coast that we never seem to experience the devastation caused by these monster storms. (Though our neighbor, North Carolina, does.)

Anyone who has watched the news in the last decade has seen the devastation caused by the increasing number of storms hammering the coastal areas of the Southern and Eastern United States. Many are seeing their waterfront dreams crumble in a heap of sticks and broken bricks. Insurance claims have threatened homeowners' ability to afford, or even obtain, insurance.

The constant threat to safety and property is driving many inland to find safer waters. And many are discovering it here and at other mountain lakes. Smith Mountain Lake has been largely unaffected by storms of any type for as long as I can remember.

What about tornadoes? I have lived here for many years and only recall one tornado in this area. Perhaps it is due to the Blue Ridge Mountains, which are about as far from Kansas as Dorothy could ever imagine.

In general, the climate here at Smith Mountain Lake is very pleasant. Due to the mountains and lack of swampy land here, it does not get oppressively hot in the summer. However, unlike Michigan, where I lived for 10 years, I can take my boat out in the winter if I choose to. In fact, I showed lots by boat in December and January to now happy Smith Mountain Lake property owners.

Section VIII: SML – A Great Place to Own Real Estate!

I Love to Sail or Want to Learn. Are there Areas of the Lake that are Better for Sailing?

Do you like to sail? There are sections of Smith Mountain Lake that probably boast the best sailing in this region. However, there are other areas on the lake where sailing would be difficult due to the width of the channel and wind patterns. If you plan to sail, be sure to confer with experienced local sailors before buying a home.

If you find your dream home, and it is not in a good area to sail from, you may be able to dock your sailboat from a nearby marina such as Pelican Point Yacht Club.

Pelican Point is in Union Hall, on the south side of the Blackwater channel. It offers about a half-mile of shoreline and 134 deep-water slips as well as a great clubhouse, swimming pool, tennis, shuffleboard, picnic areas, a boat ramp, and boat and trailer storage. They are also brokers for used 22- to 36-foot sailboats.

Is There a Warm Side Versus a Cold Side of this Lake?

I used to think this was an odd inquiry. Was this a trick question? Then I learned that many other man-made lakes, such as Lake Anna here in Virginia, have a nuclear reactor on their lake. These reactors push hot water from their cooling towers back into the lake, and they can even heat up a whole side of a lake. While this sounds nice for swimming in the off-season, it just...well...gives me the creeps! I'm fine with nuclear power generation, but I don't want a nuclear reactor next door to my vacation getaway. I will put up with the cold water in November! (Smith Mountain Lake is a producer for hydroelectric power – the way God intended it! ☺)

Section VIII: SML – A Great Place to Own Real Estate!

How Could Global Warming Affect Vacation Properties in the US? How Will This Affect Smith Mountain Lake?

National Geographic (see November 2004 article at http://news.nationalgeographic.com/news/2004/11/1109_041 109_polar_ice.html) states the following: "The rising temperatures are likely to cause the melting of at least half the Arctic sea ice by the end of the century. A significant portion of the Greenland ice sheet -- which contains enough water to raise the worldwide sea level by about 23 feet (about 7 meters) -- would also melt...The consequences of such a massive meltdown of northern ice would be dramatic, according to the study...Low-lying coastal areas in Florida and Louisiana could be flooded by the sea. A 1.5 feet (50-centimeter) rise in sea level could cause the coastline to move 150 feet (45 meters) inland, resulting in substantial economic, social, and environmental impact in low-lying areas."

A Natural Resources Defense Council report (Global Warming Threatens Florida – this report was originally accessed on the web in 2008 at **nrdc.org/globalwarming/nflorida.asp**) states the following: "Global warming, an increase in the earth's average temperature caused by a build up of heat-trapping gases in the atmosphere, is often regarded as an abstract threat. But 'Feeling the Heat' details global warming's real-world effect on life in Florida, moving the climate-change discussion from the abstract to the specific.

Among the threats global warming poses for Florida's people and resources:

- As glaciers melt and warming waters expand, sea levels will rise anywhere from eight inches to two-and-a-half feet over the next century. In Florida, seawater will advance inland as much as 400 feet in low-lying areas, flooding shoreline homes and hotels, limiting future development, and eroding the state's beloved beaches.

- As salt water encroaches inland, freshwater supplies feeding Florida's cities, agriculture, and tourist centers will be at risk of saltwater contamination.

- Saltwater encroachment will also likely inundate coastal wetlands, gravely threatening the lower Everglades and its wildlife.

- Tourism will likely suffer. Sea level rise, climbing temperatures, and alterations in rainfall will combine to damage beaches, the Everglades, coral reefs and other unique ecosystems that make Florida such an appealing tourist destination.

- Global warming will pose specific health threats to Florida's citizens, likely increasing the incidence of heat-related illness, exacerbating poor air quality, and perhaps even making it easier for infectious diseases to spread. Florida's seniors will be particularly susceptible to these effects.

- The impact of global warming on agriculture may not be felt at first; indeed, it is possible that climate and water conditions will help some commercial crops in the short run. But it's likely that climate changes will lead to lower yields of such important cash crops as citrus, sugarcane and tomatoes.

- Forest wildfires are very likely to be more common, and do more damage -- the result of higher temperatures and more intense droughts -- although the magnitude of this effect will depend on overall changes in rainfall. Also, global warming may increase the threat to forests from

Section VIII: SML – A Great Place to Own Real Estate!

invasive species and pests." (End of quote from Florida global warming report.)

This may not seem like an imminently big deal to you. You may think that it will not have a significant effect on a coastal investment property in your lifetime. I don't believe this is necessarily an accurate perspective, however. Anyone familiar with stocks or other related markets knows that the value of investments is based first on news and perceptions of the future. If this is all true, there will come a day when the market shifts, when widespread fear takes hold of investors and property owners, and when For Sale signs are numerous and buyers nowhere to be found. I cannot imagine the effect this will have on coastal properties everywhere.

I don't know when this day will come, if ever, but I do know this: Smith Mountain Lake is suspended 795 feet above the current level of the world's oceans. If global warming raises the sea level a few feet, I think that we will still be alright! If and when this panic does happen, I predict that it will have a two-fold effect on Smith Mountain Lake. For one thing, new buyers may be looking inland to find their vacation properties. Secondly, I can imagine that investors in droves will be leaving their waterfront properties in coastal areas coming inland to places like Smith Mountain Lake.

I hope this never happens. I am not predicting that it will. I am just attempting to interpret the potential situation. There are conflicting reports, so I don't know if global warming is real at all. Furthermore, I don't know if global warming will ever really have an effect on property values in coastal areas. Millions of people do believe it, however, and this is bound to have an impact on property values. It may happen in the blink of an eye. It is this widespread *perception* that may ultimately result in this shift. If this tragic situation plays out this way, waterfront property owners at Smith Mountain Lake would ultimately be perfectly positioned, both geographically and financially.

Is Smith Mountain Lake a Profitable Place to Invest?

Real estate investment at Smith Mountain Lake can be a profitable way to increase personal wealth. You may think, as I once did, that buying a second home is too costly or frivolous, that it is a stretch to make it work within your investment and retirement plan. But there are many reasons that buying at Smith Mountain Lake may be the best investment you ever make. I have chosen to invest a significant portion of my portfolio at Smith Mountain Lake, and many others have done the same.

The retirement of the Baby Boom generation means that tens of millions of people are in the process of finalizing their plans to make their big move in the coming years. The majority of Americans live in the East and will likely remain in this part of the United States upon retirement. It is no secret that a significant proportion of these retirees are looking to live by the water or in the mountains. They want to slow down their pace, yet they still wish to enjoy the culture of nearby cities.

Smith Mountain Lake truly has all of this and much more. Every year we hear the same comments over and over. Recently, a couple from Pennsylvania who found Smith Mountain Lake on a map scheduled a two-day visit to check out the area. They had been looking all over the Northeastern seaboard for a place to spend their golden years. Their trip turned into six days. They bought a beautiful waterfront lot, and their home is underway. They said they never imagined it would be so beautiful here. It's people like this that are causing SML to grow in popularity every year.

Did you ever consider why the retirement of the Baby Boomer Generation is so significant to the value of resort properties like those offered here? Statistics say the Baby Boomers have the greatest wealth of any group in the history of the world. One reason for this is the significant income earned by these individuals in recent decades. Much of this has been

Section VIII: SML – A Great Place to Own Real Estate!

plowed into retirement plans that will be available soon. Many people think that there is no better use for these funds than to purchase a place to enjoy and continue to see it grow in value.

A second reason for this Baby Boomer wealth is the growth in home equity during recent decades. Even with the downturn we experienced, the facts are that home equity generally increased over the past decades. I regularly interact with clients who bought a home for around a few hundred thousand that is worth close to a million dollars now.

Another often overlooked factor is the release of massive funds through inheritance. Statistics say that $8 trillion (eight with 12 zeroes) is being inherited from the passing of the World War II generation in one decade. Amazingly, these funds are being received by the same people with the wealth in retirement plans and home equity! These are the same people who often want to live near water and mountains...often in the Eastern US.

All marketers know that massive revenue will be generated wherever the baby boom population arrow is pointed. In the 50's, it was Gerber baby food. In the 70's, Levi Jeans. In the 90's it was mutual funds and VHS players. Now the arrow is pointed directly at retirement and expensive recreation. This is why Warren Buffett, who looks at 20-year trends when investing, recently bought one of the world's largest RV manufacturers. And multi-billionaire real estate investor Sam Zell has reportedly purchased a number of high-end RV campground properties. Do you see how Smith Mountain Lake perfectly fits this bill?

David Stevens is the former Sr. VP of Freddie Mac, former head of HUD and Deputy Director of the FHA, and now the President and CEO of the Mortgage Bankers Association in DC. David passed over waterfront properties all over the East Coast to purchase a vacation home here at SML. David said, "The Smith Mountain Lake area is a hidden gem for long-term investment value. The ability to buy waterfront property at affordable prices, on one of the most beautiful lakes in the nation, still exists at SML. With the aging population aiming towards retirement on or near waterfront in temperate climate areas, combined with the unique timing right now of almost record low interest rates and a wonderful inventory to choose from, buying a home at SML...may prove to be one of the wisest investment opportunities for real estate available in the mid-Atlantic or Southeastern US." The pieces of the puzzle fit together well. Does it make sense for you to contact us to discuss investing at Smith Mountain Lake? I hope you'll call or email us today.

Section VIII: SML – A Great Place to Own Real Estate!

Smith Mountain Lake Versus the Beach

We have been discussing the unparalleled investment potential of waterfront property at Smith Mountain Lake. Another reason for this is a simple fact that many are now becoming aware of. Well, it's actually not a fact, but it is the opinion of a growing number of people who want to live on the water...

Lakefront living has MANY advantages over living near the ocean!

I will detail many of the reasons for this, but for now, since we are discussing investments, let me give you one simple reason. In general, oceanfront property became popular decades before lakefront, so the prices at the ocean skyrocketed to (often) many times that of lakefront homes. In the last decade, the popularity of lakefront property has exploded as well. But it is still not as fashionable as oceanfront...yet. As a result, the appreciation potential of a lakefront home is greater, in the opinion of many investors, than that near the beach.

One person who helped clarify this for me was the man I mentioned above, David Stevens, the former head of HUD, and one of the most astute individuals in the nation on real estate trends, especially as they affect the financial markets. For years David had been looking for a second home at the Outer Banks, and was very pleased with the value of similar homes here at Smith Mountain Lake. He said the home he purchased here would cost many times more on the water in the Outer Banks. After spending a number of vacations here, he also realized that there was actually more of what his family really wanted to do here!

One of the reasons he gave is the opportunity to have a powerboat, jet ski, canoe and sailboat just a few steps from his back door. Though this may be remotely possible in rare situations in an oceanfront setting, this is the norm for homeowners here at Smith Mountain Lake. My dock and boathouse area include a Hurricane deck boat, a Hobie Cat sailboat, my friend's wakeboard boat, two Sea Doos and a canoe. My neighbor on one side has a paddleboat for more leisurely rides and the other neighbor has a fishing boat.

David said his family didn't want to spend big money and time docking their crafts at a local marina, as he would at the ocean. This is a hidden cost that many don't think about when making a comparison. The convenience of having these vessels right at hand has provided David – and countless others here – the joy of a true waterfront experience.

Another reason that many now prefer SML to the ocean is the absence of hurricanes here in Southwestern Virginia, as I discussed elsewhere.

Since I wrote the first edition of this book, one of its readers wrote me an email on this topic. He said:

Paul,
Another selling point of lake vs. ocean. The salt water is much more harmful to the metals and finish on houses and water vehicles. I have to rinse my boats off after each use or pay a price in engine repairs and extra wax.
Patrick Stover
Annapolis, MD

I hadn't thought of this one, and I guess it isn't something one would think of unless they were living it. Thanks for the tip, Patrick!

I believe that Smith Mountain Lake holds many advantages over oceanfront living. I admit I am a little biased – but so are thousands of others from New England to California!

One of my recent lot buyers has lived in seven or eight locations around the nation. He currently lives in a beautiful home near San Francisco. He was part of successful software company that went public and his wife is vice president of a national retail chain. He called me last summer and said that in all of his travels he'd never seen a place like Smith Mountain Lake, and though he could afford to live at the ocean or in the mountains, this is where he wanted his residential journey to end. His family had visited here only briefly while living in

Section VIII: SML – A Great Place to Own Real Estate!

North Carolina years before, yet they decided that this is where they would one day build their retirement home.

He informed me that he was prepared to spend up to $1.5 million on a premier waterfront lot here with deep water, privacy, a direct view of the mountains, and a nearly flat building site. After going back and forth for months online and via phone, he traveled here for four days.

On day one, we took a boat tour of the lake. With map in hand, we surveyed the various features and home styles of the different sections of our "Jewel of the Blue Ridge." We enjoyed a great view of many lots from the vantage point that only the water can give. On day two, we went by car and got a different view of the various waterfront lots that we had narrowed down in previous months. By sunset, we narrowed it down to the top four. On day three, we rented a private plane and flew over the lake, getting a breathtaking aerial perspective of the waterways, neighborhoods and lots we had been reviewing.

My new friend was more impressed with the lake than he had previously imagined, and was especially pleased that he was able to go home with a lot that exceeded his expectation at a little over half of what he anticipated from California. He has now told other Bay area residents of our beautiful secret and I am preparing to take his friends on a similar tour here soon.

David and my new West Coast friend are thrilled with their property purchases at Smith Mountain Lake. Are you ready to enjoy a similar experience? If you want to join people from all over the United States who now call this home, please contact a local Smith Mountain Lake REALTOR® today.

Come to the Mountains...

Have I convinced you that life here at Smith Mountain Lake, for many of us, exceeds the life that we could enjoy in many other resort areas? I have discussed the ability to enjoy a dock by your back steps, the opportunity for various types of boating and swimming within earshot of your living room, the lack of hurricanes and other weather problems, the peace and solitude here, and the vote of confidence we are getting from second-homeowners, vacationers, investors and retirees from all over the nation. Lower costs of living are mirrored by low crime rates and a slower pace of life.

There is one other thing we enjoy that can't be experienced at any oceanfront destination I know of in the Eastern United States. Mountains...beautiful Blue Ridge Mountains! I am aware that there are many beautiful destinations in Washington and Oregon with mountain vistas rising from rocky shorelines, but I have not seen any place in the Eastern United States with the mountain/water beauty that we enjoy here at Smith Mountain Lake.

If you haven't been here, I am hard-pressed to describe this amazing place. Rather than try, I will refer you to the photo gallery on our **SmithMountainHomes.com** website. These photos, however, are actually a meager representation of the beauty we enjoy here at Smith Mountain Lake. The only way to really enjoy it is to see it in person.

Have you scheduled a trip here yet to look around? Is there anything we can do to assist you? I hope that you will contact us today to see if Smith Mountain Lake real estate is in your future. We look forward to meeting you!

Appendices

What's in This Section?

Appendix A: A Brief History of Smith Mountain Lake

Appendix B: How Electricity is Produced at Smith Mountain Lake

Appendix C: From You to SML - Drive Times & Distances

Appendix D: Smith Mountain Lake in the National Media

Appendix E: When Smith Mountain Lake Won't Satisfy

Appendix F: The Dreamer's Challenge

Appendix A: A Brief History of Smith Mountain Lake

Early History – Colonial Settlement

In 1720, two new counties were formed in the Virginia Colony: Spotsylvania in the north and Brunswick in the south. Brunswick County was eventually divided into smaller counties, which were further divided and reapportioned until the three counties that now define the lake were formed. Settlers quickly embraced Spotsylvania County, but development in Brunswick County was slow to take off. This can be attributed to the fact that most settlements in Virginia followed existing natural waterways, which were necessary as trade routes. The rivers that define this area all flow into North Carolina rather than to ports in Virginia. Thus, in order to send goods to Virginia ports, roads would have to be built, and this was no small task.

By 1738, the colonial government had seen enough, and took decisive action. It was decreed that *"any person who within ten years shall settle upon the Roanoke River, on the south branch (Dan) above the fork; and on the north branch above the mouth of the Little Roanoke and all lands lying between shall be exempt from all levies (taxes) for ten years...and that letters of naturalization be granted to any alien settling there, upon taking the oath of parliament."*

These aliens included Quakers from Pennsylvania, who had fled persecution in England to settle in the New World. Among those intrepid souls were Daniel and Gideon Smith, brothers for whom the Mountain, and eventually, by extension, the lake were named. Just like many of us today, they arrived from another state, coming here to escape high taxes. In 1740, the Smith Brothers laid claim to thousands of acres and made their homes here.

Other early settlers were Scotch-Irish and German, mostly from Pennsylvania, and those family names are still common

Appendices

here. Others who came for the tax break were from Eastern Virginia. Although the 10-year tax-free period has long since expired, newcomers to Smith Mountain Lake still enjoy the benefit of relatively low tax rates, even when compared to cities as close by as Roanoke and Lynchburg.

Recent History – Into the 20th Century

Original plans for what is now Smith Mountain Lake began as early as 1906, when a hydroelectric dam was first proposed here. In 1925, the site of the present dam was purchased by the Roanoke River Navigation Company. This company had originally been chartered to find ways to improve the ability to move cargo to seaports in North Carolina. With customary government swiftness, the project was studied, discussed, then largely ignored until 1934, when the Army Corps of Engineers once again picked up the baton.

The Smith Mountain Project was a part of the larger overall plan. The Corps was concerned with flood control, a major problem in the Roanoke River Basin, as well as the generation of electric power. Priority was given to other parts of the plan, particularly Buggs Island and Gaston.

In the meantime, opposition to the construction of the Smith Mountain Dam was raised by officers of the Norfolk and Western Railroad, whose principle revenues were derived from the shipment of coal. These men feared that a hydroelectric dam would reduce the need for coal, thereby cutting deeply into their bottom line. Executives of Appalachian Power (APCO) joined in the protest, claiming that the project was neither practical nor advisable, again laying bare their fears of competition from a government-subsidized electric utility.

A major point of contention was that the original plans and studies all called for the Army Corps of Engineers to build the dam, as they had done in numerous other locations. Public hearings were held, including one in Moneta, where opposition to government competition with private enterprise was said to be a step toward socialism. The tipping point was finally reached when Appalachian Power applied for a permit to privately construct the dam. Supporters of the project were just as happy, as long as the dam would be built. Finally, in 1958, permits were issued to Appalachian Power to construct both the Smith Mountain and Leesville Dams.

The next step was to acquire the necessary land. In order to create the resultant lakes, APCO had to purchase the acreage they would encompass. Company trucks began canvassing the countryside, making purchase offers to landowners. Typical offers were about 30 dollars per acre. Although there seemed to be no mention of eminent domain, affected residents were apparently given little choice.

Claude Holland of the Franklin County Historical Society has lived in this area all of his life. "You talk to a lot of people, you're going to get different stories," he said when asked about the land transfers. He asserted that in some cases, money was just deposited in the bank and people were told to leave. Some were reluctant, but one way or the other, all of the land was eventually acquired. Some blessed landowners had acreage extending above the lake's fill line. In such cases, part of the family farm was retained, and soon became waterfront property.

Holland also mentioned that some parcels had been abandoned, in some cases because of the steep slope, which rendered it practically valueless. APCO was able to acquire these parcels simply by paying the back taxes. Ironically, over time, some of these tracts became quite valuable indeed.

With title to the necessary acreage in hand, the next step involved dotting the landscape with little red flags, marking the 800-foot (above sea level) contour. Once in place, these markers were used as guides for the removal of trees, brush, buildings, and anything else that lie in a swath below the 795-foot contour. The swath was logged, bulldozed, and burned until it was completely clear. Any buildings or personal property had to be removed by the owners if they wished to keep it. Anything of value could be salvaged by the previous landowner prior to flooding the land. Most property owners removed everything

Appendices

valuable. Some houses, or parts thereof, were moved to higher ground. Others were left in place, but stripped of most items of value. No clearing was done below the 765 foot contour. Longtime lake residents like to regale listeners with tales of water skiing between the trees as the lake was being filled. Once the lake reached 765 feet, any remaining growth that protruded above the water was lopped off.
While landowners did their part to remove all their property, another problem remained. The land that was about to become lake-bottom was dotted with scores of family cemeteries, some of which had become overgrown with vegetation. These cemeteries were identified and the remains removed and re-interred elsewhere. A total of 68 cemeteries, including 1,135 graves, were relocated from the Smith Mountain reservoir. Graves dates as far back as 1750. According to the records, 673 of the relocated graves were of white people, and 688 were described as "colored," many of whom had been slaves. The remains were re-interred into 27 different nearby existing cemetery sites.

Power Source or Vacation Resort?
I wasn't here when the lake was developed, of course. However, we all hear stories, and different storytellers have different perspectives. It seems that a lot of local folks were cynical about the lake when it was developed. No surprise. My friend's father was one of the old farmers who vigilantly held out and apparently had to be taken to court by the power company over a matter of their access on his property. He held out until the year of his death in 2003. I heard about other farmers who were trading their new lakefront property for other land to get as far away from the lake as possible.
  Few people seemed to be thinking about the lake as a real estate opportunity back then. Recreation perhaps, but not real estate. There were some entrepreneurial, development-minded

The Definitive Guide to Smith Mountain Lake Real Estate

folks who had a vision for the value of the property, but it would take decades for the real estate market to really take off. I recently talked to one REALTOR® from nearby Roanoke who sold lots at Smith Mountain Lake in the late 1960's. Now in his mid-80's and no longer involved at the lake, he said, "We were selling nice waterfront lots for about $1,500 each (yes, fifteen-hundred!). At one point, we raised the price on some of the nice, flat point lots to $2,500 and they called us crooks!" He went on to say, "I'll bet that some of those lots sell for over $100,000 dollars now." I replied, "Yes, sir, that is true. And the ones you're describing probably sell for over half-a-million dollars in many cases."

In the early years of development, most people could not see the point of wasting the money to construct a full-fledged house here on the waterfront. Trailers, small cabins, cottages, and cinderblock homes were the norm in those days. Some forward-thinking folks constructed larger homes, however. Many of those homes that remain are considered "tear-downs" now, being demolished for the value of the lot and replaced with large, impressive structures.

Smith Mountain Lake has come a long way in these 50+ years, and we are excited to see how it will look in the next 50. Perhaps you will be a part of helping shape the future of this mountain-lake paradise that more and more of us are calling HOME each year.

Information for "A Brief History of Smith Mountain Lake" is drawn from two articles in *Discover Smith Mountain Lake* **Magazine by Timothy Ernandes titled** *"Lake Lore: What's in a Name?"* **(January-June 2007 Issue) and "What Lies Beneath?" (July-October 2007 Issue)**

Appendices

Appendix B: How Electricity is Produced at Smith Mountain Lake

Operation of the project makes maximum use of one of our natural resources – water – through a process called pumped storage. Water stored in Smith Mountain Lake first drops through the turbine generators in the Smith Mountain Dam power house to produce electricity. Instead of allowing all of the spent water to run away downstream, much is caught and held by Leesville Dam, the lower dam in the project, to be pumped back into Smith Mountain Lake later for re-use. A portion of the water goes through turbine-generators at Leesville, generating additional electricity.

SMITH MOUNTAIN PROJECT OPERATION
Smith Mountain is a pumped-storage project that utilizes an upper reservoir (Smith Mountain Lake) and a lower reservoir (Leesville Lake). The water stored in Smith Mountain Lake first passes through turbine-generators in the powerhouse to produce electricity and is then discharged into Leesville Lake. Most of this water is retained in the Leesville Lake and is pumped back into Smith Mountain Lake for re-use. A portion of the water goes through the turbine-generators at the Leesville powerhouse to generate additional electricity and to meet the minimum discharge requirements of the project's Federal Energy Regulatory Commission (FERC) license.

The Smith Mountain development utilizes a 2-foot power pool. This means that when Smith Mountain generates power by passing water through the turbines, the Smith Mountain lake level can fluctuate up to 2 feet before the Leesville Lake becomes full. In other words, a 2-foot decrease in Smith Mountain results in Leesville Lake increasing 13 feet, or from a minimum elevation of 600 feet to maximum elevation of 613 feet. Once Leesville is full, power cannot be produced at Smith Mountain until some portion of the water is pumped back to Smith Mountain Lake.

There is no set schedule for operating the project. Generation generally takes place when the demand for electricity is high and water from the lower reservoir is pumped back into the upper reservoir when the demand for power is low. The operation of the project can change on an hourly basis depending on system demand.

The normal full pond elevation at Smith Mountain is 795 feet but the normal operating range under full pond conditions is considered to be between 793 feet and 795 feet because of the 2-foot power pool. Normal operating range for Leesville is between 600 feet and 613 feet. Under low in-flow conditions, the pond elevation at Smith Mountain can fall below 793 feet.

ADJUSTED ELEVATION
Lake level information can be found on AEP's website, AEP.com, under Environmental/Renewables and Energy Efficiency or by calling the automated system at 540-985-2767. The Smith Mountain fore bay level is the actual (current) level of the Smith Mountain Lake as measured at the dam. The Smith Mountain adjusted elevation is the elevation that Smith Mountain Lake would be if the water held in Leesville for re-use (between elevations 600 and 613) is pumped back into Smith Mountain. Under this scenario, when the adjusted elevation and the actual elevation are the same, the project is at its maximum power-producing potential.

The adjusted elevation is important to know because it places the current level of Smith Mountain Lake in relation to the 2-foot potential fluctuation. If the lake level and the adjusted lake level are the same, then the lake may drop 2 feet during the day. On the other hand, if there is a difference of 2 feet between the lake level and the adjusted lake level, then the lake level will not drop further because it is at the bottom of the 2-foot power pool. The Smith Mountain Project is normally considered full when the adjusted elevation is 795 feet. The adjusted elevation may be more than 795 feet during periods of high inflow and less than 795 feet during periods of low inflow.

From SmithMtn.com website – produced by Appalachian Power Company.

Appendices

Appendix C: From You to SML - Drive Times & Distances

Are you headed to or from Smith Mountain Lake on your next vacation or driving trip? Or maybe you have friends or family in other areas whom you would like to visit or persuade to come and see you. Then again perhaps you have only recently heard of our beautiful little corner of Southwest Virginia and need to know the approximate mileage in order to come visit us. Either way I hope you will find this partial list of driving times to be of benefit in your journeys. For local folks, the drive to Smith Mountain Lake is approximately 40 to 50 minutes from Martinsville, Roanoke, Lynchburg or Danville.

CITY	APPROXIMATE MILES & TIME
Atlanta, GA	466 miles - 7 hours
Baltimore, MD	272 miles - 5 hours
Blacksburg, VA	60 miles - 1.5 hours
Charleston, WV	225 miles - 4 hours
Charlotte, NC	190 miles - 3.5 hours
Charlottesville, VA	105 miles - 2 hours
Chicago, IL	700 miles - 14 hours
Cincinnati, OH	460 miles - 9 hours
Columbus, OH	375 miles - 8 hours
Detroit, MI	624 miles - 10 hours
Greensboro, NC	105 miles - 2 hours
Knoxville, TN	290 miles - 6 hours
Lexington, KY	385 miles - 7 hours
Nashville, TN	465 miles - 9 hours
New York, NY	505 miles - 10 hours
Norfolk, VA	225 miles - 4 hours
Philadelphia, PA	358 miles - 6 hours
Pittsburgh, PA	365 miles - 7 hours
Raleigh, NC	128 miles - 2+ hours
Richmond, VA	150 miles - 3 hours
Washington, D.C.	220 miles - 4 hours
Winston-Salem, NC	110 miles - 2 hours

Appendix D: Smith Mountain Lake in the National Media

Note: For copyright purposes, the following articles are not reproduced here in their entirety. See SmithMountainHomes.com/News for more information.

The New York Times
In Virginia, a Blue Ridge Retreat That Is a Little Undiscovered
By ROBERT STRAUSS
June 22, 2007

This article is the most significant piece that has been produced about Smith Mountain Lake. It paints a very favorable picture of the lake, the region, the local folks and those who have moved or purchased second homes here. Real estate agent Rob Gerner is quoted in the article: *"Smith Mountain Lake has that odd combination of nothing and everything to do. There aren't really places to go clubbing or that many organized events,"* said Rob Gerner, who attended the University of Virginia in the mid-1960's, moved to the region in the late 1970's and became a real estate agent there. *'People tend to just use the lake in whatever way possible. They fish or boat or water-ski. They hike. They sit out and look at the scenery. It's not a fast life here, just a good one...You come here even in May and there may only be 50 boats out on the lake. We're still a little undiscovered.'"*

The article states: *"Smith Mountain Lake has 500 miles of shoreline, with mountain and water views almost everywhere. The lake is clean and accessible from many docks, both private and public. Roads may be rural and most often two-lane, but they are rarely clogged. People tend to eat at home, so

Appendices

restaurant lines are almost nonexistent. Property taxes are low — about $1,500 on a $300,000 house — because there are few schools to support."

The article paints a favorable picture of the real estate market and the availability of homes and property here at the lake.

USA Today
April 20, 2006
10 Great Places to go Float Your Houseboat

Dust off your navigational charts, skippers: It's only a month until Memorial Day weekend, which kicks off the most popular season for houseboating. Whether you own a houseboat or want to rent one, it's a great way to get together with family and friends — or just get away. North America's most popular (and therefore populated) houseboating waters are Lake Powell in southern Utah and Lake Cumberland in Kentucky. Consider these recommendations from Houseboat magazine's managing editor, Brady Kay, who spoke with Anne Goodfriend for USA TODAY...

#3 Smith Mountain Lake
Southwestern Virginia

Nestled in the Blue Ridge Mountains with 500 miles of shoreline, the lake celebrates its 40th anniversary this year; it was made by damming the Blackwater and Roanoke rivers to generate electricity. The closest cities are Roanoke (west of the lake) and Lynchburg (east). "For houseboating, it's calm, and there are lots of places to rent boats." Besides, with hordes flocking to Washington, D.C., for summer vacations, Smith Mountain Lake — a four-hour drive away — "gives the tourists a respite from sightseeing." 800-676-8203.

See *www.usatoday.com/travel/destinations/10great/2006-04-20-houseboating_x.htm* for the latest rankings.

HGTV's House Hunters Special Episode
Press Release – June 2008
Smith Mountain Lake Home buyer and REALTOR® to be Featured on HGTV's House Hunters Reality Series

HGTV's House Hunters show will feature Smith Mountain Lake in its upcoming "waterfront week" this June. Pie Town Productions, producers of the popular reality TV series, selected Smith Mountain Lake from a large number of potential lakefront destinations. Paul Moore, who is a local agent with Wainwright and Company REALTORS®, as well as his client, who is currently undisclosed, will be featured on the show.

"I was hiking with my son in the mountains when I first received a call from Pie Town," Moore stated. "I was a bit stunned, to say the least. They said they were doing a weeklong special of waterfront homes to include oceanfront, river, beachfront and a lake home. Smith Mountain Lake was chosen from all the lakes in the U.S. as the lake destination for the show."

The producers had searched the web for a lake with panoramic scenery and a variety of waterfront homes. Katie Hall, field producer for the show, found Moore's website, **SmithMountainHomes.com**, which features a variety of lake information and a striking photo gallery. "They were impressed with the mountains and beautiful water in the photos of Smith Mountain Lake, but they were stunned when they viewed the lake in person during their shoots onsite last fall," Moore said.

After in-depth conversations with Moore, the producers selected him as the agent for the Smith Mountain Lake segment. The

Appendices

next step was to locate the right home buyer. "They wanted a couple who typified home buyers here at the lake. This was tough since we serve clients from different walks of life all over the Eastern United States. But they all share a passion for fresh water, a rural lake lifestyle and our dazzling Blue Ridge Mountains," Moore said.

It happened that Moore's Smith Mountain Homes Realty Team was working with a couple from the Washington, D.C. area who seemed to be a perfect fit. "They own a number of D.C.-area businesses, and they were searching for a waterfront home on the lake in Bedford County," Moore said. He talked to the couple and they jumped at the opportunity.

The next step was for the couple to submit a home video to the producers. The video they submitted showed the couple giving a tour of their D.C. home and businesses. "The producers agreed that they were a perfect fit, and they showed up with a camera crew a few weeks later."

House Hunters first filmed the couple at their D.C. home and then followed them on a search for their weekend getaway home at Smith Mountain Lake. The episode features them looking at three competing homes and, in the final moments, revealing which one they selected.

The show highlights shots of the lake and community from the ground and by boat. "I am honored to be part of the show, but I am most excited that the rest of the world will see the beauty of our somewhat undiscovered mountain-lake paradise," Moore said.

Chris Flint, Tournament Angler
http://www.chrisflintfishing.com/blog/smith-mountain-lake-virginia/

"If during a dreary North Country spring you feel the need for a break, Smith Mountain Lake VA may just be the place for you. There is beautiful water there with breath taking backdrops of the Blue Ridge Mountains and some of the nicest people on earth!"

Game & Fish Magazine

September 30, 2010
http://www.gameandfishmag.com/fishing/fishing_crappies-panfish-fishing_va_0408_01/

Slab Crappie Tactics for Smith Mountain Lake

"Though not necessarily known for its numbers of crappie, Smith Mountain might just be a sleeper when it comes to hauling in big slabs." ~Phillip Gentry

Nestled in the Blue Ridge Mountains of southwestern Virginia, Smith Mountain Lake comes to mind when most Virginia anglers think of either largemouth or striped bass fishing...From a crappie angler's point of view, the structure of the lake makes things a little easier than in some lakes.

"A lot of Smith Mountain's crappie are caught in secondary channels and bays off the Blackwater and Roanoke River arms," said Dan Wilson, biologist for the Virginia Department of Game and Inland Fisheries. "Beginning in April, depending on water temperatures, crappie begin staging in the mouths of these secondaries and will make their way toward the backs of the areas looking for spawning cover."

Appendices

Lake Lubbers
July 2011 Newsletter
America's Most Popular Vacation Lakes
http://www.lakelubbers.com/newsletter-07-2011.html

20,600-acre Smith Mountain Lake, "Jewel of the Blue Ridge", is located in the foothills of southwest Virginia's Blue Ridge Mountains. Smith Mountain Lake is the home base of Lakelubbers. SML hosts special events throughout the year, including bass tournaments, fireworks on the water, a wine festival, fall chili and craft festival, charity home tour of lakefront homes, and a Christmas boat parade Smith Mountain Lake State Park and Franklin County Park feature beautiful sand beaches and miles of hiking trails. The parks, plus five golf courses, provide plenty of opportunities for outdoor recreation. The paddlewheel cruise ship, the Virginia Dare, offers scenic lunch and dinner cruises. With 500 miles of shoreline to explore, Smith Mountain Lake welcomes all types of watercraft, speedboats, pontoon boats, bass boats, jet skis, canoes and kayaks. And watch for the Fall 2011 release of the new movie, Lake Effects, filmed entirely at Smith Mountain Lake.

USA TODAY
August 2, 2013
10 Great Places to Go Bass Fishing
http://www.usatoday.com/story/travel/destinations/10greatplaces/2013/08/01/10-great-places-to-go-bass-fishing/2610967/

James Hall, editor of Bassmaster Magazine, shares some favorites from the magazine's list of the top 100 bass-fishing lakes.

#4 Smith Mountain Lake Virginia
"You don't usually find good smallmouth and largemouth bass fishing in the same area, but this Blue Ridge Mountain reservoir near Roanoke is blessed," Hall says, "with plenty of 3 or 4 pound fish. You can catch not only both species, but you have really good quality."

From *Best Place to Retire* Website:
Retirement Living in Smith Mountain Lake – Virginia
best-place-to-retire.com/retire-in-smith-mountain-lake-va

Located in central Virginia along the Blue Ridge Mountains, Smith Mountain Lake is considered to be the Jewel of the Blue Ridge. It is equidistant from Roanoke and Lynchburg. Only a 4-hour drive southwest of Washington D.C. and two hours north of Raleigh, NC, at Smith Mountain Lake you'll find wonderful places and people.

Our area's great natural beauty--from the waters and woods to the Blue Ridge Mountains of Virginia--is the perfect destination for your very own style of fun, whether you seek activities or just plain relaxing.

Appendices

Appendix E: When Smith Mountain Lake Won't Satisfy

The great philosopher and author C.S. Lewis once posed the question, "What does it tell me when I find within me a desire which nothing in this world can satisfy?"

As we have discussed elsewhere, Smith Mountain Lake contains most of the great elements of beauty and wonder this world has to offer. Blue Ridge Mountains, clear water, rolling meadows, relaxing sunsets – a world of wonder right at your doorstep. It stands far apart from my former fast-paced life in metro-Detroit, and I am so thankful to be here.

And yet I notice in myself, and in others I talk to, that it's just not enough. I see the excitement in my clients' eyes when they find that perfect waterfront home, and while I am thrilled to be a part of the process, I know there will ultimately be some letdown. Haven't you noticed this, too? Has there ever been a car, a home, a boat, a toy – any experience that *really* left you overflowing with joy...permanently? Was your expectation before your marriage completely fulfilled after the honeymoon, or was there an element of disappointment? Though you may thoroughly enjoy your vacation, your career or your children, do you ever lie awake at night and wonder if this is all there is? Do you ever wonder if this is all you were created for? I know that I have.

Why are fairy tales so popular in all civilizations in all ages? After achieving his life-long dream of winning the World Series, why did baseball great, Kirby Puckett, sit in the locker room and ask, "Is this all there is?" What causes a man to throw away his family and his legacy for one night with a stranger? What motivates us to continue to buy bigger toys, more expensive vacations and cars that go nearly triple the speed limit?

The great mathematician, scientist and philosopher, Blaise Pascal, wrestled with these types of questions and he concluded that there is a hole in the heart of every man and woman. "It is a God-shaped hole and it will never be filled except by the One who placed it there." St. Augustine said, "Our hearts are restless 'til they find their rest in Thee."

We were created by an intelligent Designer, and it only makes sense that He designed within us a longing that nothing on this earth can satisfy. He designed us with a deep hunger for Him, a hunger to know Him personally, to know His thoughts, His desires, and His plans for our lives. He designed us with a void that can only be filled by something, or actually Someone, who is currently invisible and mysterious, One whose thoughts and ways are infinitely greater than ours. I can confidently state that the longing in your heart and mine is a longing for the One who created us. I know this because He says it clearly in His Word, the Bible.

His Word also makes it clear that there is an infinite gap between us and Him, a gap that was not supposed to be there, a gap that we caused through our rebellion against our Creator. Every single one of us, from Adolph Hitler to Mother Teresa and all of us in between, are in the same predicament, and we are all naturally destined for eternal separation from our Creator as a result. Having rebelled against an infinite Being, we have committed an act of infinite rebellion, and we have therefore incurred infinite punishment. (Sorry, I didn't write the mail – I'm just delivering it.)

The greatest news of all time is that He sent His Son, Jesus, the Infinite One in human form, to pay the infinite price for our rebellion and offer us the fulfillment of the life that we've always longed for, the dreams we've dreamed but never understood, the joy that will never end on this earth or forever. However, this offer requires a response from each one of us. It is not enough to think lightly about something of eternal significance or to just hope you're good enough to make it. Most of us give more thought to the purchase of our second home on earth than we give to our eternal home where we will dwell forever, in endless misery or perpetual joy.

Appendices

So what about you? Have you determined the answer to the ultimate question in life?

C.S. Lewis said, "Creatures are not born with desires unless satisfaction for those desires exists. A baby feels hunger – well, there is such a thing as food. A duckling wants to swim – well, there is such a thing as water. Man feels sexual desire – well, there is such a thing as sex. If I find in myself a desire which no experience in this world can satisfy, the most probable explanation is that I was made for another world. If none of my earthly pleasures satisfy it, that does not mean the universe is a fraud…earthly pleasures were never meant to satisfy it, but only to arouse it, to suggest the real thing." (C.S. Lewis as quoted in *Things Unseen* by Mark Buchanan, pg. 54.)

You and I were indeed created for another world, and nothing on this earth will ever satisfy our deepest cravings until we joyfully submit our lives to our brilliant Designer and loving Father.

Appendix F – The Dreamer's Challenge

I feel compelled to add one more appendix. This is a very personal note on a topic that I have come to understand between the second and third editions of this book.

I realize this could sound manipulative, or like some clever sales pitch. I hope you know that is not my intention in the least. In fact, the possibility that I may be misunderstood in that way tempts me to push delete on this whole section right now. But I'm willing to take the risk, with the hope that this will resonate with some of you and you will come to experience something you were created for but perhaps never lived out.

If you read the previous section, you realize that I'm very passionate about our Creator and His desire for relationship with His people. For years, I have known him as a Redeemer, who came to rescue people. And technically as a Father.

But more recently I have come to *really* understand Him as a good Father who cares about every detail of His children's lives. Like the very best earthly father, but infinitely better.

I grew up believing that God was not interested in our wants, but merely our needs. I felt as if my natural desires were in a tug of war with His greater, more spiritual plans. I don't believe this anymore.

If it's important to you, then it's important to Him.

God is a loving Father. He's also brilliantly creative. And you were made in His image. So creative expression is a natural outflow of the fact that He was looking in a mirror when He created you. (Have you ever thought of that? See Genesis 1:26.)

I have an employee who loves big cities. He relaxes in a noisy café on a crowded street. I have a daughter who loves solitude and feels at home in a forest. Some find beauty in a desert. Others on a beach.

If you are drawn to a lovely mountain lake…

Appendices

Have you considered the possibility that your love for mountains and lakes may have been deposited in you by a loving Father? Has it dawned on you that He will be pleased... even *delighted*... when you mirror His creativity by finding and creating a mountain retreat that will bring great joy to you and your family, and provide a place for friends to gather and create memories that will last a lifetime and beyond?

There is a supernatural power involved in our desires. For those who walk in an intimate relationship with their Creator, He says, "I will grant you the desires of your heart" (Psalm 37:4). I don't know how this works all the time, because sometimes I don't get my way. But isn't it true that you can often look back on what you *thought* you wanted and realize you got something far better?

For years I thought that denying my desires would be noble and selfless, but now I see things differently. I have now made one of my goals to delight the heart of my Father by fulfilling my divine purpose. I do this, in part, by embracing the role of creative expression consistent with the fact that I'm made in the image and likeness of a loving Creator.

So if this resonates with you, what's a possible next step?

Matt McPherson was struggling to make ends meet. Trying to support a wife and five children on a limited income wasn't working out for him, and he had an irresistible passion for bow hunting. In fact he was on a tight budget, and was trying to build a compound bow in his spare time.

One day, Matt sensed he heard God whisper this in his mind: "I have the best ideas for every problem in the world. I would tell people if they would just ask me."

Now Matt could have asked for the solution to world hunger. Or global warming. But he didn't. He said this to God: "Well if you have the best ideas for everything, can you show me how to build a better bow?"

It sounds crazy, but Matt reports that two weeks later, he had a vision. In the vision, there was a pencil sketch of a completely new design for a compound bow. He copied it down, and long story short, he built it, launched a new company, and now runs one of the most profitable sporting goods companies in the world.

Honda sells a lot of cars, and makes a moderate profit on each. Mercedes sells fewer cars, and makes a lot on each. Mathews Archery sells an enormous volume of bows and makes an enormous profit on each one.

Do I hear you saying, *"Hold on, Paul. Why would God care about that? What about human trafficking and the droughts that plague Africa?"*

Like I said before, "If it matters to you, it matters to Him." He has infinite bandwidth, and we are His Plan A. We are the only creatures on earth that are positioned to fully express His ingenious creativity and His loving compassion. So it makes sense that he would download His best ideas to us. To you.

He doesn't hide things from you. He hides them for you.

Every Easter, my wife and I enjoy hiding eggs for our family and others we celebrate with. We hide some eggs right in plain view, right by the sidewalk, and the older kids understand that these are for the little ones. My friend, Jack, and I enjoy finding crazy places to hide others. Some end up in crooks of tree branches and wedged behind car tires.

If we hid all the eggs for older kids in plain sight, they would be discouraged. No fun in that. "C'mon! Try a little harder, dad!"

But what if I jumped on a backhoe, dug a five-foot deep hole, dumped the eggs on the bottom, and covered it with concrete? Then I said, "Have at it, kids. Good luck." Then I went inside to watch TV. That would be even less fun, and you would think I was cruel or crazy.

Appendices

I don't do either one, and in fact my wife and I find that our delight is *in the kids' delight* in finding what we carefully hid *for them*. And our kids' delight is in *our delight* in them enjoying the whole process. I'm made in the image of God, and my best fathering is but a faint reflection of a good, good Father. ***He's better than we think, so we need to change the way we think.***

So what's this all have to do with Smith Mountain Lake?

I don't know you, but you have apparently read this far. I propose that a good, creative, loving, joyful Father has placed a seed of creative expression in you. And *perhaps* that expression is hinted at by a desire that He placed in your heart. A desire for beauty, and family, and the creation of memories that will last forever. A desire that *possibly* includes a mountain-lake retreat at our lake or any of dozens of other beautiful lakes or mountain retreats in North America.

The Dreamer's Challenge

Many who are reading this have not found that place yet, and perhaps you are starting a search for that perfect home now. If that's you, I have a simple challenge:

> *How about putting God to the test? How about asking Him to show you the perfect spot? How about envisioning what your dream home would include and asking Him to lead you to the perfect one? And to lead you in some way that is inexplicable without supernatural intervention.*

Maybe it's a place that's not even for sale yet. Maybe it's a home you drove by and you'll happen see to the owner in the yard, or you'll have the courage to go to their front door. Maybe it's someone your broker sold to in the past, and your desire to buy and their timing to sell fit together perfectly now. Just ask Him. And see what happens. He loves you, and He loves to reveal more about His nature. He longs to fulfill your desires and to partner with you to create a corner of Earth that looks a lot like Heaven.

I'd love to hear the outcome, and I may even post your dream story on my website with your permission. Email me at **paul.moore@SmithMountainHomes.com.**

HAPPY DREAMING!

About the Author

After graduating with an engineering degree from Marietta College and an MBA from Ohio State, Paul entered the management development track at Ford Motor Company in Detroit. He later departed to start a staffing company with a partner. Before selling to a publicly traded firm five years later, Paul was Finalist for Ernst & Young's *Michigan Entrepreneur of the Year* two years straight.

Paul and his family moved to the Smith Mountain Lake area a year later to enjoy a more rural lifestyle and assist a growing church. They also started a nonprofit ministry to international students studying at US colleges. Paul re-entered the business world in the real estate arena in 2000. After only two years as a REALTOR® at Smith Mountain Lake, he achieved the Diamond Award, the highest sales level for a Roanoke Valley/SML realty agent. Through applying principles of direct response marketing and Internet technology, his Smith Mountain Homes Team has sold tens of millions of dollars of SML real estate to hundreds of now-happy SML property owners.

In recent years, Paul joined a team of entrepreneurs, educators, and pastors to form 7MountainSchool.com. The 7 Mountain School holds an optimistic view of the future for America and the world, and trains young people to move boldly into various spheres of society to bring positive, lasting change.

A large portion of the profit from Paul's business is funneled into 7 Mountain and other world-changing initiatives. These include putting orphans in homes, ending human trafficking, and raising the standard of living for the impoverished around the world.

Attention SML Home Buyers:

> **Purchase Your SML Dream Home through the *Smith Mountain Homes Team* and Get a Free Home Warranty!**

This is an exclusive offer for readers of The Definitive Guide to Smith Mountain Lake Real Estate. Here's how it works:

If you're **not** currently working with an SML REALTOR®, show this page to one of our top-notch *Smith Mountain Homes Team* agents. Let our agent work with you to locate your waterfront dream home here at Smith Mountain Lake.

When you close on your new home or condo, we'll pick up your one-year home warranty. This is about a $400 value, and it covers most of the things that could go wrong in your home, like:

- Air conditioning and heating units
- Refrigerator, Oven, Dishwasher & Hot Water Heater
- Plumbing and electrical wiring systems

We'll help you locate your waterfront dream home...and our gift of a Free Home Warranty will cover most major repairs for a year.

So please contact us today!

1-877-SML-HOME
paul.moore@SmithMountainHomes.com

Attention SML Home Sellers:

After the recent economic downturn, many homeowners are curious about the current value of their SML area home. Whether you're ready to sell your home or not... and if you're even a little bit curious...

Get a Free Market Analysis of Your SML Area Home!

This is an exclusive offer for readers of The Definitive Guide to Smith Mountain Lake Real Estate. Here's how it works:

If you're **not** currently working with an SML REALTOR®, show this page to one of our *Smith Mountain Homes Team* agents. We'll perform a thorough market analysis on your home. This will include:

- Listing & Sales Stats for All Your Neighbors' Homes
- The Most Likely Sale Price for Your Home Today
- A List of Best Staging Ideas for Your Home

Knowledge is power. After receiving this evaluation, you'll know how your home has weathered the downturn. And you'll have the knowledge to make important decisions about next steps.

There's no other obligation.

So please contact us today!

1-877-SML-HOME
paul.moore@SmithMountainHomes.com